Courage AND Hope FOR EVERY DAY

180 readings to strengthen your spirit

Carolyn Larsen

Revell

a division of Baker Publishing Group
Grand Rapids, Michigan

© 2019, 2020 by Carolyn Larsen

Published by Revell
a division of Baker Publishing Group
PO Box 6287, Grand Rapids, MI 49516-6287
www.revellbooks.com

Combined edition published 2022
ISBN 978-0-8007-4097-9 (hardcover)
ISBN 978-1-4934-3434-3 (ebook)

Previously published in two separate volumes:
Words of Courage for Women © 2020
Words of Hope for Women © 2019

Printed in the United States of America

22   23   24   25   26   27   28   7   6   5   4   3   2   1

words of courage

for Women

1

The Source of Courage

Surely God is my salvation;
  I will trust and not be afraid.
The LORD, the LORD himself, is my strength and my
    defense;
  he has become my salvation.

ISAIAH 12:2

Why does fear take root in your heart? Are you afraid you can't withstand temptations or that you won't be able to stand against Satan's attacks? When you invite Jesus into your heart, he becomes your strength to stand against all frightening things. He becomes your shield against danger and your defender against all enemies.

God promises in his Word to always be with you. Read that again: *always!* He's the source of your courage. Allow his strength to fill your heart so you can face whatever is before you. Never doubt his power because, after all, he promised it to you.

What can you do when anxiety threatens to paralyze your heart? Push the fear away by focusing on God. Read Scripture. Remind yourself of how he has strengthened and protected you in the past, and remind yourself that his powerful presence is still with you. Step confidently into your day, and refuse to cower in fear.

Start each day by renewing your courage through the quietness of prayer and through rest in God. Ask him to fill your heart with an awareness of his power and presence and to bolster your courage through that knowledge.

2

Perfect Love

> *There is no fear in love. But perfect love drives out fear, because fear has to do with punishment. The one who fears is not made perfect in love.*
>
> 1 JOHN 4:18

ear is an interesting emotion. Even when you try to have courage, fear wiggles its way into your heart, similar to the way water manages to leak through the smallest opening. A little anxiety is certainly normal because life does have its tense moments and . . . you're human. However, all-consuming fear and trust in God's love cannot exist in your heart at the same time. If you truly believe that God loves you, why are you afraid?

God's love is perfect. What does that mean to you? Perfect love is deep, pure, constant, steady, forgiving, trustworthy, dependable, protective, sacrificial, and a multitude of other adjectives. Perfect love . . . there is nothing wrong with it and nothing to criticize about it. Grasping, believing, and trusting in God's perfect love for you helps push away fear because you know God is protecting you and guiding your decisions and steps. He loves you perfectly, so there is no reason to fear. Take courage in his love. Ask God to help your love for him grow deeper so that you have a greater understanding of his care for you.

3

Guarded

You hem me in behind and before,
and you lay your hand upon me.
PSALM 139:5

You've probably seen photos of celebrities out in public, surrounded by security guards they've hired to protect them. They have a wall of guards around them to make certain no one gets too close. The guards protect their employer on all sides and constantly evaluate the crowd for any situation that might bring danger to them.

Maybe you can't afford to hire bodyguards to protect you wherever you go. But here's some news: you have the best bodyguard imaginable—God! The psalmist says God is in front of you and behind you. Nothing and no one gets close to you without God knowing about it. And not only is he protecting you in front and in back, but he also has his hand on your shoulder, guiding your steps and making sure you don't fall, much like a loving parent who helps a child cross a busy street.

It is amazing to know that God loves you so much that he protects you, guards you, and guides you. He cares about what happens to you every moment of the day. When anxiety begins to rear its ugly head, remember that you are well guarded. Trust your Bodyguard!

4

The Love of a Father

The Spirit you received does not make you slaves, so that you live in fear again; rather, the Spirit you received brought about your adoption to sonship. And by him we cry, "Abba, Father."

ROMANS 8:15

Not every human father is a good father, and if you haven't had a good father, that may influence how you perceive God as Father. If that's true for you, read the following description of God as your good Father:

> Your good Father wants the best for you. Yes, sometimes that may mean he disciplines you because that's what a good father does in order to help you learn and grow.
>
> Your good Father watches out for you. He does all he can to protect you, day in and day out.
>
> Your good Father delights in you. He enjoys your laughter. He takes pleasure in your enjoyment of all he

provides for you, from the world he has made to the friends and family he has given you. Enjoy it all!

Your good Father is forgiving. Don't be afraid to confess your sins to him. He won't turn away in disgust. He won't turn away at all. He forgives you and offers a multitude of opportunities for you to get life right, even as he teaches and guides you.

You needn't ever be afraid of your good Father; in fact, you can be brave and courageous in the knowledge that you are your Father's child and that he loves you more than you can imagine.

5

Just for This Time

If you remain silent at this time, relief and deliverance for the Jews will arise from another place, but you and your father's family will perish. And who knows but that you have come to your royal position for such a time as this?

ESTHER 4:14

It takes courage to tackle some of the challenges that come your way in life. Some of those challenges arise from tasks God calls you to handle. Has God given you a job that feels too big or too dangerous or even beyond what you have the capability to accomplish?

Queen Esther felt that way. The task before her was very dangerous. She could have been killed for doing what she was asked to do. If she was successful, she would save the Jewish nation. If she wasn't, they would die and so would she.

What can you learn from Esther? She accepted the challenge but asked her people to pray for her. She didn't go into the challenge without their prayer support. Esther accepted the reality that facing this challenge might have been the very reason God put her on earth: "For such a time as this."

God has a purpose for your life—work he wants you to do for his kingdom. He won't send you into that work without walking beside you and equipping you with what you need. The prayer support of others certainly strengthens you too. You aren't alone, so be courageous and go boldly into what God calls you to do.

6

The Hardest Thing

Wait for the LORD;
be strong and take heart
and wait for the LORD.
PSALM 27:14

re you familiar with the expression "like a bull in a china shop"? It's a description of someone who rushes into situations without thinking things through, without preparing adequately, or without having all the information. Rushing into anything in this manner seldom ends well.

When a crisis arises in your life or when a difficult situation is in front of you, is it your tendency to rush in and try to handle things yourself, without God's guidance or power? Sure, you pray, but if God doesn't move or direct you quickly enough—well, waiting is hard. In fact, one of the most difficult things God may ever ask you to do is . . . wait.

It takes courage to wait for God. But waiting means you trust him. It shows that you believe he will either handle the situation or give you wisdom and direction to know what to do. Even if the crisis goes on for a long time, you wait because you trust him.

Do you want to know how courageous you are? Do you want to test how strong your faith is? Then wait on God's guidance, and wait on his action.

7

Courage to Face Temptation

No temptation has overtaken you except what is common to mankind. And God is faithful; he will not let you be tempted beyond what you can bear. But when you are tempted, he will also provide a way out so that you can endure it.

1 CORINTHIANS 10:13

Temptation is a part of life. Certainly not a pleasant part, but still a part. There may be certain temptations that cause you to be especially anxious because you know they are hard for you to resist. But here's the thing: there is no temptation you face that hasn't been faced by others in the past or that won't be faced by people in the future. And you won't face any temptations that God doesn't already know about. He knows absolutely everything that comes into your life.

What can you do to be able to look temptation in the face and not be afraid? How can you have the assurance that you will be able to withstand temptation? The best thing to do is to ask God for help. Ask him for strength, wisdom, and guidance. Then pay attention to how he answers your prayer. Don't expect him to take the temptation away, because he knows your faith in him will grow stronger as you trust his strength to help you stand up to the temptation. Through his help, you will find the courage to face the temptation, and your faith will grow stronger and deeper because of it.

8

God's Restoration

The God of all grace, who called you to his eternal glory in Christ, after you have suffered a little while, will himself restore you and make you strong, firm and steadfast.

1 PETER 5:10

You will undoubtedly experience problems at one time or another in your life. But, instead of being discouraged by them, remember that these things can serve to make you stronger. Search the words of Scripture to be reminded of God's presence and care for you. Focus on the lessons you're learning and how your dependence on God is growing stronger because of your experiences. It's true that there are struggles in life and that you have an enemy trying to pull you away from God.

But have courage! You're not in the battle against Satan by yourself. God is paying attention and is ready to strengthen and protect you. Call on him to help you get through your troubles. He wants to help your faith grow stronger and deeper. When you experience his power and restoration after you've struggled and suffered, your trust will grow deeper. Then you can face with courage any problems that come, because you know God is with you and he won't let the troubles you face destroy you. So go forward with courage. See God's hand in your life. Trust him to be there for you!

9

What's Your Goal?

Consider it pure joy, my brothers and sisters, whenever you face trials of many kinds, because you know that the testing of your faith produces perseverance. Let perseverance finish its work so that you may be mature and complete, not lacking anything.

JAMES 1:2–4

When you invite Jesus into your heart, you become a child of God. Great, but that's not the end of the story. You want your faith to grow stronger and deeper. You want to know God more intimately and become more dependent on him, because you believe you can trust him with your very life and with everything that matters to you.

How does your faith grow stronger? You know that learning a new language requires a great deal of study and practice. Developing new athletic skills takes hours of practice and often means muscle pain. Are you seeing the message here? Learning something new takes work. Faith grows stronger when you exercise it, and that happens during hard times, when your faith is tested. Is it fun or easy? No, of course not. But when you face problems and trust God to help you through them, you are persevering. So commit to staying close to him, leaning on him, and letting him guide you through your problems. As you see him leading, strengthening, and guiding, your faith muscle will grow stronger because you will know he is always with you and you can trust him no matter what. And with that trust, as James encourages, you may become mature and complete, lacking nothing!

10

Peace and Courage

You will keep in perfect peace
those whose minds are steadfast,
because they trust in you.

ISAIAH 26:3

Your thought life can take you on some interesting journeys if you let it. It will take you on the "What if this happens?" journey and the "Why didn't I do this or say that?" trip. If you depend on your thought life to be a trip advisor or a planning tool, things will seldom turn out well. Peace will not be the outcome.

However, there is a way for peace to be the foundation of your life.

Keep your thoughts settled on God. Make him and his Word the filter that all other thoughts pass through. When anxiety and fear start to wiggle into your thoughts, stop and pray. Read God's Word. Focus on Bible verses that remind you of God's presence and his immense love for you. Remind yourself of ways he has protected you and guided you in the past. Refuse to let the what-if thoughts take control of your mind. Allow your trust in God to push them away. Remember the many times he has shown you how very much he loves you and has proven that he will take care of you.

Keeping your thoughts locked on God because you know that you can trust him gives you courage to face whatever life brings. It also gives you peace as you go through difficult times.

World-Changing Courage

When they saw him walking on the lake, they thought he was a ghost. They cried out, because they all saw him and were terrified.

Immediately he spoke to them and said, "Take courage! It is I. Don't be afraid."

MARK 6:49–50

What's your reaction when God does something incredibly amazing? How do you feel when you see the majesty of his creativity and strength in nature? Are you a little frightened at his power and greatness? (The disciples were.) Does the scope of his might that's available in your life entice or frighten you?

When you come face-to-face with the power of Jesus through circumstances, through nature, through your own heart, don't be terrified. Instead, let that experience make you aware of the infinite power available to you through your relationship with him. His power will change you, change lives, change the world. Are you ready for that? The disciples were terrified because, when they saw him walking on top of the water, they didn't know what to think about his control.

Jesus told them, "Take courage! It is I. Don't be afraid." Hear him say that to you, and let the possibilities of his power in your life give you courage to exercise a risk-taking faith that will be used mightily by God!

12

Courage to Love Others

Love your enemies and pray for those who persecute you, that you may be children of your Father in heaven. He causes his sun to rise on the evil and the good, and sends rain on the righteous and the unrighteous.

MATTHEW 5:44–45

At some point in your life, someone may become upset with you. You may even have an enemy because of someone's perceptions of you or because of something you've said or done. How do you respond to someone who is upset with you? Do you get angry in response? Do you bad-mouth that person? Do you try to get others on your side of the situation? Or do you love . . . just love?

It takes courage to love someone who doesn't love you back. It takes courage to even be kind to someone who may not receive that kindness well. But you must remember whose child you are. Your powerful heavenly Father will give you the courage to speak a word of kindness. He will give you the strength to lift your hand—not so you can strike out at the other person, but so you can shake their hand, give them a pat on the back, or even give them a gentle hug.

Yes, loving those who don't like you is hard. It means taking a risk, so it takes courage. That courage comes from the powerful love of God in your heart. Ask him to help you love your enemies. He will fill your heart with courage.

13

Courage to Heal Relationships

Do not repay anyone evil for evil. Be careful to do what is right in the eyes of everyone. If it is possible, as far as it depends on you, live at peace with everyone.

ROMANS 12:17–18

Relationships are wonderful. Families, spouses, and friends—life would be pretty boring without them. But once in a while stress creeps into your relationships, which may cause you to react or respond in a way that isn't the best. It takes courage to admit when you haven't behaved your best. When you have an issue with another person, the temptation is to be self-protective or even to get a little revenge. But that's not the way to emulate God's love to others, is it? Keep in the forefront of your thoughts that your responsibility is first and foremost to be an ambassador of Jesus Christ by your words, attitudes, and behaviors.

Step forward with courage and admit your personal failure in the situation. Ask forgiveness. Reestablish communication. Make it your goal, as the apostle Paul instructs, to live at peace with others. It will not always be easy. It will sometimes mean sacrificing your feelings and living humbly. When you need help to do this, ask God for strength and to help you see situations from a viewpoint other than your own.

14

Courage to Share Your Faith

Jesus came to them and said, "All authority in heaven and on earth has been given to me. Therefore go and make disciples of all nations, baptizing them in the name of the Father and of the Son and of the Holy Spirit, and teaching them to obey everything I have commanded you. And surely I am with you always, to the very end of the age."

MATTHEW 28:18–20

Before he went back to heaven, Jesus instructed his followers to tell others about God's love. Do you find it scary to speak about your faith to another person? Do you have trouble finding the right words? Are you nervous that people will reject your message—or that they'll even reject you?

The news of God's love is the best news ever, but it takes courage and sensitivity to share it with others. If you don't share your faith, people you care about may miss out on the best news ever given and the blessing of knowing God. That means they could miss the blessing of eternity in heaven. This is serious, so you must believe the importance of your message. If you need courage to share your faith, ask God to help you share his love with those he brings into your life. He will give you opportunities, the right words, and a deep passion to share his love. Your courage should come from the last part of these verses in Matthew: You're not on your own to share your faith—Jesus is with you. Always.

Focused on God

Look to the LORD and his strength;
seek his face always.

1 CHRONICLES 16:11

When you're afraid, where do you turn for help? Do you turn within? To friends? To power? To money? To success? Wherever you turn indicates what you feel is most likely to calm your fear. It shows where you're putting your trust. Where is the focus of your heart and mind?

When you need strength and courage, the only solution that offers true hope is God. His strength is without measure. His power is beyond comprehension. The ocean waves obey him. Weather obeys him. He is the Creator of everything, and his power is greater than anything else on earth.

Whatever help you need, whatever part of your life in which you are struggling with waning strength, God is the answer. Put your trust in him to guide you and help you with any challenges life brings your way. Keep your heart always turned toward him. Don't let anything push God out of the number one position in your heart and thoughts. Other things will constantly try to usurp his position, but be careful that nothing becomes more important than God's love and approval in your life. Your faith will grow stronger and deeper as you see you can trust him in every aspect of your life.

16

Love Song

The LORD your God is with you,
the Mighty Warrior who saves.
He will take great delight in you;
in his love he will no longer rebuke you,
but will rejoice over you with singing.
                                        ZEPHANIAH 3:17

God is with you. Nothing will happen to you today that he doesn't already know about. He will walk with you through whatever difficult, frightening experiences come along.

It's safe to say that God saves you multiple times even in one day because he's watching over you. He keeps your foot from a false step; he stops your car in time to prevent an accident. Does he stop every single crisis? No, but he gives his presence so you're never alone.

God doesn't just save you, he celebrates you. It gives him joy to be with you, to give you things, and to do things for you. Think about that—the Creator of everything in the universe actually delights in having you close to him.

He forgives the sins you commit and the times you push him to the background. Accept his forgiveness, and also forgive yourself and move forward in your life with him.

Lastly, realize that God himself is singing a love song over you, for you, because of you. So be courageous in your walk with him. Love him with abandon because that's how he loves you!

17

Courage When You're Discouraged

My dear brothers and sisters, stand firm. Let nothing move you. Always give yourselves fully to the work of the Lord, because you know that your labor in the Lord is not in vain.

1 Corinthians 15:58

Having courage means being brave, having nerve, being daring. There's strength in the word *courage*. The word *discouraged*, while it has the same root word, means downcast, disheartened, and dejected. There's weakness in this word.

You may get discouraged when you're doing God's work—whether that means parenting as a Christ follower, living a godly example before an unbelieving spouse, being a Christian employee, or serving as a professional in Christian ministry. You may sometimes feel as though you're failing, or you may get discouraged because you see no progress. It can be hard to persevere.

Trust the apostle Paul's words here so you don't get discouraged. Nothing you do for the Lord is ever in vain. While it's true that you may not see the positive results of your efforts for a long time (or even in your lifetime), you can trust that your work is laying a foundation in someone's life. Someone else may add the next layer for that person, but be assured that every word you spoke, every helping hand you offered, every prayer you prayed will be used by the Lord. So keep serving with love and intentionality. Have courage in sharing your faith and in doing God's work because he *will* use everything you do for his kingdom!

18

Be Prepared

Put on the full armor of God, so that you can take your stand against the devil's schemes.

EPHESIANS 6:11

What are you struggling with? Relationship issues? Too many commitments? Parenting? Temptation? How are you going to win these battles? They might look like normal, everyday battles, but they are attacks by Satan to pull you away from God. That's his goal. But God has provided all the protection you need to fight off Satan's attacks. The protection is there. You just have to use it.

Putting on the armor of God takes an intentional effort on your part. He has provided it, but you must take action. Some pieces of the armor may be difficult to put on and practice faithfully—for example, the one that covers your thought life and choices. Satan plants thoughts that make you doubt God's care, thoughts that lead to judgment and criticism of others, and thoughts that make you question your self-worth. You know where your weakest point is, so concentrate on preparing yourself for battle by putting on that piece of armor.

Once you have prepared yourself for life by putting on the armor of God outlined in Ephesians 6—the truth of who God is, righteousness, readiness, faith, and salvation—you will be prepared and protected by what God has provided, and you can courageously and powerfully face whatever life brings.

19

Courage While Waiting

They will have no fear of bad news;
their hearts are steadfast, trusting in the LORD.
PSALM 112:7

When you undergo medical tests, you must then wait for the results. The waiting is the hardest part. You're in a holding pattern. You try to keep your mind away from what the results might be. You try not to think about the what-if questions. You try to have courageous faith.

It's okay to be afraid. Whether you're awaiting the results of a medical test or you're dealing with another issue, the road ahead is unknown and it very well may not be easy. However, you can certainly trust that nothing will happen to you without God knowing about it first. You can know that your trust in him will take you to a deeper, more trusting faith, and that kind of growth comes only through trial and testing. Whatever your test results may be, you will not have to go through even one second of the journey alone. God is walking with you, holding you close, loving you, and teaching you every step of the way. Find courage in a deeper, more intimate relationship with him. Let his courage fill your heart.

20

Uniquely You

There are different kinds of gifts, but the same Spirit distributes them. There are different kinds of service, but the same Lord. There are different kinds of working, but in all of them and in everyone it is the same God at work.

1 Corinthians 12:4–6

Do you ever feel boxed in by others' opinions or expectations of you? People can pigeonhole you to be a certain way, to behave a certain way, and even to serve God in a certain way. Once you've slid into a certain niche and stayed there for a while, it might be scary to try something new. Sometimes that's fine. But what if God wants you to try something new? Are you courageous enough to step into that?

God has given you certain gifts to use in certain ways to serve him. Don't get caught up in doing what you've always done if he is nudging you to do something new. Don't look at someone else and wish you could be just like them. Be courageous enough to be the real you and to serve God and others through that realness. God will work through you to accomplish whatever he calls you to do. Look for the adventure of the new and unique. Be willing to try new things, and see where God leads you!

21

Taking On the Big Guy

David said to the Philistine, "You come against me with sword and spear and javelin, but I come against you in the name of the LORD Almighty, the God of the armies of Israel, whom you have defied."

1 SAMUEL 17:45

You may know the story of young David rising to the challenge of a giant named Goliath who was armed with a shield and spear, while David had only a slingshot and a few stones. David wasn't afraid. He knew he could win. God was on his side, so he knew he could defeat the big, powerful, well-trained giant. He was right. Nothing and no one is stronger than God.

What "Goliath" are you facing in your life? A job change? Relationship struggles? Health issues? Finding your way in life? Changes in your life situation are challenges for sure. It takes courage to face them and keep moving forward. Where does that courage come from? God himself. Remember that the Lord Almighty is fighting for you. Stop and think about his power displayed in creation and his control over the wind, rain, ocean, and all of nature. Think about how God interacted with his people in Scripture—especially in the Old Testament. His power is immeasurable. His strength is unmatched. His love for you is unconditional. Take courage to face whatever your Goliath might be, because the Lord Almighty, the God of the armies of Israel, is fighting for you!

Courage in the Dark

*Even though I walk
    through the darkest valley,
I will fear no evil,
    for you are with me;
your rod and your staff,
    they comfort me.*

PSALM 23:4

When children are afraid, they want to be close to someone they trust, someone they know will take care of and protect them. They feel safe when they're with certain people, and they gain courage from that closeness. Any monsters or bad guys they might perceive to be in the darkness are minimized by the presence of someone they trust to protect them.

You have an even more powerful bodyguard walking through life with you: God. Life may take you through some very dark valleys with tall cliffs on either side that hide the sunlight. But the thing is, you don't walk through those valleys alone. Your loving Father goes before you and follows after you. He guides your every step, even when you can't see solid ground ahead of you. He protects you from anything that could sneak up from behind to destroy you. He comforts you in the pain of the journey. He whispers to your heart, "You can do it. You can make it. Keep going." He cares about what you're going through. Knowing he's with you gives you courage to keep moving forward one step at a time.

23

The Rubber Meets the Road

Do not let your hearts be troubled. You believe in God; believe also in me.

JOHN 14:1

If you've accepted Jesus as your Savior, then you have confessed that you believe he is truly the Messiah, God's Son. You believe that he was present at the creation of all there is. You believe his power, strength, and wisdom are greater than any other power, strength, and wisdom.

But where the rubber meets the road—in other words, where the honesty and depth of your faith come into play—is at a point in your life when you face a crisis that sends you into a spiral of fear and worry. How you react to troubles shows your true opinion and feelings about your faith.

Jesus says that if you truly believe in him, you can trust his power, strength, wisdom, and love. Complete trust that leads to powerful courage is the goal. Does this happen easily? Not necessarily. But each time you push fear aside, trust him, and see his response, your faith grows stronger. Each time you cry out to Jesus for help, your belief deepens. Faith is a journey. Learn from each experience, and your courage will deepen as your fear fades away in the realization and experience of Jesus's love and power.

24

Take a Risk

When she heard about Jesus, she came up behind him in the crowd and touched his cloak, because she thought, "If I just touch his clothes, I will be healed." Immediately her bleeding stopped and she felt in her body that she was freed from her suffering.

MARK 5:27–29

This woman's story is told in just a few verses in three of the Gospels. She suffered from a bleeding issue for twelve years. She spent all her money on doctors, to no avail. Her condition made her unclean, which may have kept other people away from her so they wouldn't become unclean too. She could have given up, but she didn't. She took a chance by going into a crowd of people following Jesus. She pushed her way past people who wouldn't have wanted her to touch them. Why did she do this? Because she believed that if she could just touch Jesus's clothes, she would be healed. That would be enough. It was.

51

How courageous is your faith? Are you willing to push your way through people or situations that are difficult in order to get closer to Jesus? Do you believe that Jesus's power is so strong that (figuratively) touching his clothes by keeping your heart focused on him and choosing to trust him no matter what will get a response? Remember what Jesus said to this woman: "Daughter, your faith has healed you. Go in peace and be freed from your suffering" (v. 34). Have a courageous faith!

25

Courage to Forgive

Bear with each other and forgive one another if any of you has a grievance against someone. Forgive as the Lord forgave you.

COLOSSIANS 3:13

Forgiving when you've been wronged—intentionally or unintentionally—is hard, especially if the person who hurt you doesn't apologize or show some repentance. In this situation, forgiving means pushing aside your own feelings and allowing God to help you forgive and to mean it. This is when forgiving takes courage.

Remember that whoever hurt you is just a person . . . as you are . . . and you know that you sometimes make mistakes, that you're sometimes selfish, that you sometimes simply do not pay attention to how your words or actions impact someone else.

Remember, too, that your anger is holding you prisoner. The energy it takes to stay angry is hurting only you. Forgiveness frees your heart to love and give and enjoy.

Where does God come into this? You will need his strength working in your heart to help you forgive. Let go of your anger. Let go of your self-centered focus, and let God help you forgive. Remember that he forgives you over and over for your shortcomings and failures. He does so willingly and lovingly. Let him give you the courage to extend forgiveness to others. In doing that, you will find freedom from your anger.

26

Courage to Walk Away

The LORD is my light and my salvation—
whom shall I fear?
The LORD is the stronghold of my life—
of whom shall I be afraid?

PSALM 27:1

Sometimes people come into your life who seem to be good for you; however, eventually you see that particular relationship is not healthy for you. Perhaps the interactions with this person are damaging to your self-esteem. Or, even more serious, they could be damaging to your relationship with God. It will take courage to step away from this person. It can be frightening. Where do you get the courage? It comes from knowing that God is on your side. He loves you very much, and his desire is for your relationship with him to grow deeper and deeper. So if someone is intentionally or selfishly pulling you away from God, he will help you walk away from them. He will give you the courage and the wisdom to do so with kindness. And he will protect you in the process, so you have nothing to fear.

Choose God and make him your stronghold—a place that is fortified to protect those inside it from attack. When you are covered with God's protection, there's nothing to fear because he will not let anything or anyone get to you. Your courage comes from your trust that God will protect you and care for you.

27

Courage to Let Go

Offer your bodies as a living sacrifice, holy and pleasing to God—this is your true and proper worship. Do not conform to the pattern of this world, but be transformed by the renewing of your mind. Then you will be able to test and approve what God's will is—his good, pleasing and perfect will.

ROMANS 12:1–2

Most people have at least an idea of a plan for their life. But what if your hopes, dreams, and goals aren't what God has planned for you? It's hard to give up control of your own life, even when you know you can trust the One you submit that control to. God asks you to offer yourself to him, lock, stock, and barrel—holding nothing back. The apostle Paul says to do so is actually your worship of God. Why does he say that? Possibly because having the courage to let go of your own agenda and desires and submitting to what God has for you shows that you trust him completely and you honor his wisdom, strength, and omniscience.

Separating yourself from what the world says is important makes room in your heart and mind for God to shift your thoughts and desires to what he knows is truly important.

Do you trust God enough to let go of your life and follow his guiding and will for you? He has only your best interests at heart, which, of course, include the ways you serve him and others. Trust him enough to let go and follow him.

28

Courage to Ask

If any of you lacks wisdom, you should ask God, who gives generously to all without finding fault, and it will be given to you.

JAMES 1:5

You don't have to have all the answers for everything in life. It's okay to ask for help, especially from God. However, for some of us it's hard to ask for help or advice. In our pride, we want to believe we always know what to do and how to think. But life isn't that easy, so sometimes we need help from the One who has true wisdom.

God won't think any less of you for asking for help; in fact, he will appreciate your questions because they show your dependence on him and your recognition of his wisdom. The hardest part of asking for help is admitting that you need the help. Courageously put your pride aside, submit to the truth of God's omniscience, and ask him to help you form your thoughts, speak the right words, and make good decisions. He will guide your thoughts and words to reflect his own heart if you will let him. Just ask; he's waiting to help you.

29

Courage to Grieve

The LORD is close to the brokenhearted
and saves those who are crushed in spirit.

PSALM 34:18

Losing someone you love is so crushing that your heart feels deeply bruised. Any reminder of that loved one brings grief rolling to the surface. Grief is real, and it can be consuming, but it's important to go through the grieving process.

Experiencing grief doesn't mean you are weak, and it doesn't mean you don't trust God or believe he will comfort your soul. It may take courage to admit you are grieving. Ask him to give you that courage so he can touch your heart, walk with you through the grief journey, and bring you through it.

God cares about your pain and loss because he loves you. So turn to him when your heart is aching, and let him remind you of the promise of eternity with your loved one. He will bring other people near to remind you that others need your presence in their lives and that you matter to them. God will give you purpose in your life and reasons to get up and be active each day. Let your loving Father come close to you so he can comfort your grieving heart.

30

Courage to Not Judge

When they kept on questioning him, he straightened up and said to them, "Let any one of you who is without sin be the first to throw a stone at her."

JOHN 8:7

It's tempting to appoint yourself judge over other people, to decide the motives for what they do or say, or to assign the reasons for how they've behaved. Some people leap to the judgment of others without even having all the information surrounding their actions or knowing the full story of a situation. A person can get pretty arrogant about their own righteousness when they've become the judge of others.

You show courage when you admit that you've thought, said, and done wrong things as much as anyone else has. Your courage guides you to push away the temptation to judge others or view them negatively.

It takes courage to offer grace to others, especially those who seem to have no repentance or regret for what they've done. So you must ask your loving, grace-giving heavenly Father to help you remember your own sin and to fill you with forgiveness and grace toward all. Leave the work of judging others exactly where it belongs—with God. Take care of your own heart by asking God to forgive your sins and to fill you with generous compassion.

31

Fueled by Love

I am convinced that neither death nor life, neither angels nor demons, neither the present nor the future, nor any powers, neither height nor depth, nor anything else in all creation, will be able to separate us from the love of God that is in Christ Jesus our Lord.

ROMANS 8:38–39

Are you afraid of failing God? You know you're a sinner who breaks God's commands. But are you anxious about admitting that to him because you fear he will turn away from you? He won't. Nothing can separate you from God's love—not even your own sin. He loves you—no matter what. It's true that the intimacy of your relationship with God can be broken by your unconfessed sin, but a broken relationship doesn't mean his love is gone.

You are unconditionally loved by God, who himself is love (1 John 4:8 states that God is love). He sees your every thought, word, and action, and he loves the ugly stuff as well as the good stuff. Gain courage from the assurance of his love. Don't dwell on the fear of disappointing him. When you sin, acknowledge it, confess it, repent, and move forward with the confidence of his unchanging love for you. Remember that he has a high goal for you: that your faith in him will grow deeper and stronger. In that growth, your dependence on him will be fueled by trust, and your service to him will be fueled by love.

32

Power from Vulnerability

He said to me, "My grace is sufficient for you, for my power is made perfect in weakness." Therefore I will boast all the more gladly about my weaknesses, so that Christ's power may rest on me.

2 CORINTHIANS 12:9

Letting others see your failures is one of the most difficult things to do. It's hard to be vulnerable with others. Sometimes it's even hard to be vulnerable with God. Do you struggle to ask him for help overcoming sins that you don't want to admit to him?

Guess what—you're not fooling God with your silent dishonesty. Here's what you need to understand: you don't have to be perfect to come to him. God's power is working in you, helping you in the areas where you're weak. It's okay that you need him—he wants you to need him. When God works in your life, giving you strength and victory, his power is evident to you as well as to others who know your struggles. Seeing his work in your life gives you, as well as those who are watching your life, courage to trust him more readily. Be bravely vulnerable with God. Ask him for help. Let his glory be revealed through you by the way he works in your heart and life.

33

Courage to Be Still

He says, "Be still, and know that I am God;
I will be exalted among the nations,
I will be exalted in the earth."

PSALM 46:10

What image does the phrase "be still" bring up in your mind? Sitting or lying down with no movement at all? Being completely silent? Neither of those things is easy to do, at least when you're awake. Why does God say to be still? Take a look at some of the possibilities:

Be still—Stop running around and doing, doing, doing. Just stop. Sit quietly in a place where you can center your thoughts on God.

Be quiet—Even as you think about God, don't start giving him a to-do list of all the problems you want him to solve. Think about his love for you. Think about his beautiful creation. Think about his power.

Be centered—Don't let your mind begin making lists
of all the things you need to do once you're finished
being still. Psalm 46:10 says, "Be still, and know that
I am God," so keep your thoughts centered on who
God is.

Why is being still important? Because stopping your ac-
tivity, your list-making, and your requests gives you a chance
to focus on who God is and to be refreshed in your relationship with him.

Do you have the courage to stop everything and be still?
Doing so will bring great dividends in your relationship with
Christ.

34

Courage to Share Your Life with Others

Rejoice with those who rejoice; mourn with those who mourn.

ROMANS 12:15

Do you have the courage to engage in someone else's life to the point that you share in their rejoicing or their mourning? Do you have the courage to allow others into your life at the same level? It's not easy. You have to be transparent and vulnerable. Is it important to share your life experiences with others? Scripture instructs you to share with those people God brings into your circle, and he gives wisdom as to which ones to be most open with. God does this because he knows that living in community is important. Being connected with others allows you to support one another through joys and sorrows. It helps everyone know they aren't alone in life. Friendships give strength and encouragement to keep going in the struggles you face, and it's just more fun to have people to celebrate your joys.

Ask God for the courage to be open to building community by sharing your life with others and engaging in their experiences too.

35

The Future

> "I know the plans I have for you," declares the LORD, "plans to prosper you and not to harm you, plans to give you hope and a future."
>
> JEREMIAH 29:11

Perhaps you are familiar with the phrase, "Upset the applecart." It refers to everything in life being turned upside down. It's scary when life takes a turn where a job is lost or a relationship ends. The future looks pretty confusing as you attempt to pick up the pieces of your life and move on. In fact, it takes real courage to turn your eyes to the future and move on from the rubble of the loss you've experienced.

The good news is that the plans for your future are not left to chance. You can take courage in the fact that every moment and every day of your life ahead is in God's hands. He has a plan for you, so any changes that have recently "upset the applecart" of your life did not take him by surprise. Trust him to navigate your path through those changes, to take you where he wants you to be. As you trust his plan and follow him, you will see his new plan develop, and it will be good. God loves you and wants good things for your future. So keep your heart focused on God as you turn your thoughts to what's next in your life. It will be good. He promised.

36

Courage to Love Yourself

*I praise you because I am fearfully and wonderfully
made;*
your works are wonderful,
I know that full well.

PSALM 139:14

There used to be a saying floating around Christian circles: "God don't make no junk." The idea, of course, is that every person has worth because every person is created by God and made in his image. It goes right along with this lovely verse from Psalm 139.

The truth is that you are unique and wonderful. God made you the way he wants you to be. You are not like everyone else, and that's good. He gave you the personality you have. He gave you the talents you possess, the interests that pique your curiosity, your body type, your looks . . . he made you to be exactly you. Of course, you have the task of taking care of your body, your health, and your attitude. Keeping your heart focused on knowing and serving God is the foundation for doing that.

Don't let discouragement or struggles keep you from praising God for who you are. Push self-critical thoughts away and celebrate God's creativity that shows in you. Praise him for what you are learning about yourself, because the core of who you are is from God, and it is good.

37

You Matter to God

Are not two sparrows sold for a penny? Yet not one of them will fall to the ground outside your Father's care. And even the very hairs of your head are all numbered. So don't be afraid; you are worth more than many sparrows.

MATTHEW 10:29–31

Satan tries to make you doubt your value to God by saying you don't matter because you're not a "star" for God. Maybe you just wash the church nursery toys or take home the kitchen towels to throw in your own laundry. Maybe you don't teach a Bible study, but you do pick up a friend who doesn't drive so she can be a part of the study. You have many ways of serving, but Satan will try to convince you that no one notices and your service doesn't matter.

Sparrows are small, common birds. So how amazing is it that not even one falls to the ground without God knowing? Do you believe you are more important to God than even one sparrow? In fact, you're so important to him that he knows how many hairs are on your head, and that number changes daily!

Don't let Satan bury you in "I don't matter" thoughts. Call on God's power for the courage to push those thoughts away. Know that everything you do for God matters. There is no small service. You matter to him more than you could ever imagine!

38

Showing Kindness

Do not forget to show hospitality to strangers, for by so doing some people have shown hospitality to angels without knowing it.

HEBREWS 13:2

You are probably willing to help a family member or friend who needs something. You might even go out of your way to show kindness to a loved one. Are you also open to helping someone you don't know very well? Would you invite someone you don't know well to lunch? Would you sit by someone you don't know yet at a church dinner? What if by showing kindness to a stranger you are actually showing kindness to one of God's own angels, as this verse suggests?

The courage to show kindness to a stranger gives you the opportunity to show the honesty and depth of your love for God and to share his love for them. It's an exercise in loving-kindness.

If you find the thought of doing anything more than saying hello to a stranger terrifying, that's okay. You don't have to do it alone. Ask God to give you the courage you need. Ask him to direct your path toward those to whom you can show kindness. Be willing to step out of your comfort zone. God will use your kindness in amazing ways to bless others, and you will be blessed in the process!

39

Standing Bare before God

Test me, LORD, and try me,
examine my heart and my mind.

PSALM 26:2

aring your soul before God happens only after you've allowed the Holy Spirit to convict you of whether you're living in obedience to him. Are you courageous enough to do both? Standing "naked" before God and yourself, with your thoughts and motives revealed, is humbling. Of course, nothing is hidden from God. He already knows your deepest thoughts and motives. So why does the psalmist make this request? Perhaps so that, as you echo these words, you also take an honest look at your heart and motives.

God convicts you and challenges you to be more obedient to his Word because his love for you is so deep that he wants you to be the best you possible. He knows you can love and encourage others. He knows you can serve him and grow his kingdom.

Facing the condition of your heart and mind right now could be difficult, depending on your circumstances, but being honest with yourself can move you to become more intimate in your relationship with God, and that is a wonderful blessing.

40

Never Alone

The LORD himself goes before you and will be with you; he will never leave you nor forsake you. Do not be afraid; do not be discouraged.

DEUTERONOMY 31:8

When you're going through a hard time and it seems to go on for a long while, there is a temptation to feel that you're all alone and no one understands what you're dealing with. If your struggles sink you into depression, friends and family may take a step back from you because they don't know how to help. Your aloneness makes your struggle even more discouraging. But you can gain courage from this promise in Deuteronomy that reminds you that you are never really alone. God promises to be with you always and nothing you do will cause him to turn away from you. God is your Creator, and he guides each step of your life. He understands what you're struggling with. Not only does he understand your pain, he cares about your struggle.

When your struggles threaten to overtake your hope, remember God's love. You cannot even grasp how powerful God's love is for you. Allow yourself to see the ways, big and small, that he makes his presence known to you, even in your darkest times. Don't be afraid or discouraged. Stand tall and strong in God's presence, power, and love.

41

Controlling Yourself

Everyone should be quick to listen, slow to speak and slow to become angry, because human anger does not produce the righteousness that God desires.

JAMES 1:19–20

What's your behavior when you're annoyed, insulted, or angry? Are you pretty good at controlling yourself so that you don't angrily spout words that truly won't help a situation but that will definitely hurt others? Sometimes it's hard not to immediately jump to your own defense or judge someone else without having the full story.

Is your goal to reflect God's love to others so that they will want to know him too? Do you desire to honor and serve him by your words and actions? If these are your desires, your words and actions matter.

When a situation escalates and tempers flare, it takes strength to be quiet and let someone else say what they need to say rather than impulsively responding. You need strength to keep your anger from flaring up and to understand that your anger will not fix the situation or mend a relationship but will only make matters worse.

Having the courage to control your anger and hold off speaking until you know the whole story gives you the power to help defuse a situation and be the bearer of God's love to those around you.

42

Painful Times

God said, "Take your son, your only son, whom you love—
Isaac—and go to the region of Moriah. Sacrifice him there as
a burnt offering on a mountain I will show you."

GENESIS 22:2

God instructed Abraham to do the unthinkable—to sacrifice his own son to God. Abraham, with incredible faith and courage, obeyed. Abraham's obedience showed his complete submission to and trust in God. He was willing to give up something so very precious to him because God told him to.

Would you be able to obey such a command? Do you have the courage to trust God when his instructions are difficult or frightening? Can you trust him in the painful times of life?

Of course, you know the end of Abraham's story: once God saw Abraham's obedience, he stopped him from hurting Isaac, and he provided an animal for the sacrifice instead.

But God doesn't always stop terrible things from happening. He asks you to trust him with whatever comes into your life. He asks you to face it with courage because you trust him completely and you know that he can use any situation for his glory.

43

Prayer

Do not be anxious about anything, but in every situation, by prayer and petition, with thanksgiving, present your requests to God.

PHILIPPIANS 4:6

Some people become defined by their anxiety because it's infused in everything in their lives. They worry not only about the crises they are facing but also about all the what-if scenarios their minds can imagine.

The problem with constant anxiety is that it saps your strength. Power, trust, and courage fade away as anxiety rules in your heart. Some people suffer from anxiety disorders, which are beyond their control. Thankfully, medication and counseling are available to help manage those conditions. But for those who choose to worry about things, God gives the antidote: prayer. Tell God what's weighing so heavily on your heart. Ask him to give you courage and strength to face your trials. Don't forget to thank him for what you're going to learn through the experience. Trust him to guide your steps, your thoughts, your words, and your actions.

Why will talking to God about your worries lessen your anxiety? Because spending time talking with him helps you remember that he loves you very much. He wants good things for you. He promises to hear your prayers and answer them. You can trust him.

44

Deep Thoughts

May these words of my mouth and this meditation of
my heart
be pleasing in your sight,
LORD, my Rock and my Redeemer.

PSALM 19:14

The words that come flying out of your mouth reflect the true condition of your heart. You can put on an outward appearance of kindness, concern, and gentleness toward others while your heart is cruel, selfish, and judgmental. You can fool others, but you can never fool God. And you don't fool yourself either.

Make these words in Psalm 19 your prayer. Ask the Lord to help you measure your words. There will be times when you need his discernment to know that you should be silent rather than reactive. There will be times when you need his strength to be courageous enough to walk away rather than speak unkindly.

God is your Rock and Redeemer. All you say and do represents him to others. Make it your goal to not only live in a way that is pleasing in his sight but also speak and relate to others in a way that pleases him. Allow him to be your teacher as you learn to love him and others more truly and deeply.

45

Stay Focused

I keep my eyes always on the LORD.
With him at my right hand, I will not be shaken.
PSALM 16:8

o you long for courage to grow in your heart? There's only one way that can happen and that is to keep your eyes focused on the Lord.

How do you stay focused on God? You do so by reading his Word every day and spending time thinking about what it says. He will speak into your heart through his words if you will be still and listen. Remember to talk with him and tell him what matters to you and where you need his help. You will see him answer your prayers, and that will encourage you to trust him more.

Where you focus your attention impacts the direction your heart takes. Make it your goal to keep your heart firmly focused on God so that nothing else becomes more important to you than he is. Focusing on his strength, power, and love will grow your courage to stand strong for him, to stay faithful to him, and to trust him more than anything or anyone else. Your strength comes only from God, so when you are focused on him, you have courage that is based on your confidence in him. Nothing can pull you away from his love.

46

Just Believe

Overhearing what they said, Jesus told him, "Don't be afraid; just believe."

MARK 5:36

When your worst fears come true, how strong is your faith? Do you trust that God is paying attention and that he cares about what you're going through?

Jairus asked Jesus to come to his house because his daughter was very sick. Jairus was afraid she would die, and he believed that Jesus could heal her. But before Jesus could go with the worried father, some of Jairus's servants came and told him that his daughter had already died. Don't you imagine that Jairus was heartbroken and even disappointed that Jesus hadn't hurried to his house? But—because the story is never over when Jesus is involved—Jesus said, "Don't be afraid; just believe." Maybe that was hard for Jairus, but he and Jesus went to his house and Jesus raised the dead little girl back to life! No doubt Jairus's trust in Jesus grew stronger, deeper, and more courageous because of Jesus's work there.

What would it take for your faith to grow stronger, deeper, and more courageous? If you have a crushing disappointment such as Jairus had, do you give Jesus a chance to show you his power through it? Your faith will grow stronger and more courageous as you see Jesus's work in your life.

47

In the Wilderness

See, I am doing a new thing!
*   Now it springs up; do you not perceive it?*
I am making a way in the wilderness
*   and streams in the wasteland.*

ISAIAH 43:19

If you've ever lost your job and searched and waited a very long time for a new one, you know how hopeless the future can appear. It feels like your online applications and sent résumés go into some black hole, never to be seen again. It's depressing. You can even identify with the Israelites who wandered in the wilderness for forty years. Forty years without really knowing where they were going. Just wandering.

Here's the thing: like the Israelites, even when you're in the wilderness for a long time, you're not out of God's mind. He knows what's happening to you. You aren't out of his control, and he does still have a plan for your future.

God is making a new way through the wilderness. He may not let you bypass it, but he will get you through that difficult time to a place of purpose and productivity again. So step boldly into the darkness of the wilderness. Step firmly onto the path he reveals, even if he shows you only one step at a time. Move forward with the courage that comes from the assurance that God is creating a new thing and opening a new way for your future!

48

Loving When It's Hard

Love each other deeply, because love covers over a multitude of sins.

1 PETER 4:8

Love is a powerful emotion. Truly loving someone helps you overlook hurts. After all, everyone messes up once in a while. Sometimes someone who loves you hurts you, often unintentionally. Because of love you take the time to understand why the situation happened. Love, as described in 1 Corinthians 13, is patient. Love doesn't hold grudges. Love isn't selfish. Love puts others before self. Sometimes that action takes courage—courage to place your emotions in the background and to understand what's going on in someone else's heart or life.

Love does that. It overlooks moments of pain and doesn't try to get revenge. Love wants the best for the other person, even if that means you don't get what you want. Love lifts; it doesn't oppress.

God's love for you is the perfect example of the power of love. Because of his love, your sins are forgiven. Because of his love, your shortcomings are overlooked. Because of his love, he provides ways for you to learn to love him better and to love others with his true love.

49

God-Honoring Conversation

Even fools are thought wise if they keep silent,
and discerning if they hold their tongues.

PROVERBS 17:28

When discussions get heated on subjects that you have strong feelings about, are you strong enough to be quiet? Why is it important that you hold your tongue in situations like this? Because such discussions often escalate into arguments that no one can win. Feelings are hurt and relationships are damaged. Being cautious about engaging in such arguments takes courage to resist stating your opinion.

What's more important than arguing your viewpoints is showing love to your friends and neighbors. Loving others is the second greatest commandment according to Jesus (see Matt. 22:39). While it's important to take a stand for scriptural truth, it's also important to do so with kindness and gentleness and the understanding that arguing seldom changes anyone's mind.

Keep silent and be thoughtful so that relationships stay strong. God will give you opportunities to share your beliefs and opinions in private so you can have meaningful discussions.

Ask the Lord to give you the courage and strength to hold your tongue and the opportunities to speak privately with those you are concerned about. Always keep the focus of your conversations on honoring God in all you say.

50

Courage to Stand Strong

The Spirit God gave us does not make us timid, but gives us power, love and self-discipline.

2 TIMOTHY 1:7

What does your faith in God mean to you? Think about what Jesus went through on this earth so that, through him, you could have the privilege of a personal relationship with God. Is your faith important enough to you to publicly show that you value his suffering, torture, and death? Or are you sometimes flippant about your relationship with God? Are you sometimes embarrassed to call yourself a Christian because someone might be cynical about the reality of God or about your need to have him in your life? The bottom-line question is, Does what Jesus did for you matter enough that you will take a public stand for him? Will you stand for him regardless of what others say or think?

There may be times when it is difficult or even dangerous to take a stand for God, but he does not intend for you to be timid about him. He will give you the power to stand for him. He will give you a love for him that overshadows all else and the self-discipline to courageously stand for him. You will be a witness to his power and love by your courage to declare your faith in him.

51

Your Shining Life

---

*Let your light shine before others, that they may see your good
deeds and glorify your Father in heaven.*

MATTHEW 5:16

The only way people who don't know Jesus will learn about
him is if someone tells them. Scripture repeatedly instructs believers to share their faith with others—to tell them
of God's love and of what Jesus did so that they can have a
personal relationship with God.

Does it frighten you to think about actually speaking
about your faith? Are you fearful of not having the right
words to explain your relationship with God? Are you concerned about how your efforts to share will be received by
others?

The first step in sharing your faith is to let your light shine.
You do that by living your life in a way that shows God is

most important to you. Honor him with your life by obeying his commands. Share his love by showing kindness and respect to others. Give others the chance to see the depth of God's love for them through your love and through your shining life.

52

A Powerful Presence

You will receive power when the Holy Spirit comes on you; and you will be my witnesses in Jerusalem, and in all Judea and Samaria, and to the ends of the earth.

ACTS 1:8

Do you long to have real power in your life? Do you feel that you could be a better person, better spouse, better parent, better Christian if only you had power? You do have it—Jesus promised! You have the power of God's Holy Spirit to help you live in obedience to God's commands. He will give you guidance to recognize when you are being disobedient. The Spirit will spark your conscience to realize when you're making bad choices or when you could do better. He will convict you when you're living for yourself by putting your own desires before obeying God or helping others.

The Holy Spirit will guide you with the words you need to have in order to share the message of God's love and care with others. He will help you explain how important your own relationship with God is and how he has changed your life. He will use you to bring others to God.

The Holy Spirit is God's power residing in your heart. He will help you know how to pray, to live, and to speak. When you feel timid or afraid, remember his powerful, protecting, strengthening, loving presence is always with you.

53

Courageous Honesty

> The Lord detests lying lips,
>   but he delights in people who are trustworthy.
>
> PROVERBS 12:22

Honesty is very important, but is a little white lie really a big deal? Doesn't everyone pad the truth once in a while? Well, whether everyone pads the truth or not, God is not a fan of lying.

Sometimes it takes a great deal of courage to be honest and especially to be honest and kind at the same time. Being consistently honest shows your character. It lets others know they can trust you and depend on you.

While it's certainly important to be kind, it's also important to learn how to be honest in your kindness. Even little white lies can damage the trust others have in you. If you always say things like, "Yes, that song you sang was the best. You're the best singer ever!" regardless of what you feel is true, your friends will begin to not value your opinion because they won't be able to trust it.

As God's child, it is important to faithfully represent him to others by your trustworthiness and honesty. Honor God with your honesty and couch it in kindness. Be courageous enough to find a way to always tell the truth.

54

Coal or Diamonds

Blessed is the one who perseveres under trial because, having stood the test, that person will receive the crown of life that the Lord has promised to those who love him.

JAMES 1:12

Coal and diamonds both have the element of carbon in common. So what makes coal stay black and common while diamonds become beautiful and valuable? The answer: heat and pressure applied to the carbon while it's deep inside the earth.

Did you catch that? Pressure makes something wonderful out of something ordinary. Problems and pressure in your life can do the same thing if you let them. You will have problems in your life. There's no doubt about that. How you face them makes all the difference in whether they will change you for the better.

Scripture tells you that God is always with you. Nothing happens to you that he doesn't know about. He offers you strength and perseverance if you will trust him and depend on him to be the source of all you need. He asks you to trust that your difficulties and crises can draw you closer to him and strengthen your faith in him—the ultimate goal. He may not take away your problems, but he will not leave you to go through them alone. Life will bring problems, which will make you stronger and more dependent on God.

55

Courage to Try New Things

> The Lord makes firm the steps
>   of the one who delights in him;
> though he may stumble, he will not fall,
>   for the Lord upholds him with his hand.
>
> PSALM 37:23–24

I t's relatively easy to be courageous when you know exactly what you're doing and how to do it. When you're repeating a task you've done dozens of times before, or when you have a mentor working step-by-step with you, there isn't much to fear.

How do you respond when the Lord presents you with a new challenge? What if he asks you to do something for which other people will be depending on you? Do you believe that if God asks you to do something, he will guide your steps and teach you the details of what you need to know? That he will strengthen you and give you wisdom? God will equip you and guide you if you will depend on him and trust him. He will not ask you to do something hoping that you'll fail! He wants you to succeed—for yourself and for his work.

Move forward with courage, knowing that God will uphold you if you stumble. He will honor your dependence on him and redeem any mistakes you make, using them for good.

56

God Asks You to Pray

Call to me and I will answer you and tell you great and unsearchable things you do not know.

JEREMIAH 33:3

Prayer is the greatest privilege God has provided for his children. Just think about it—you can speak directly to the Creator of everything! You can go to the One who is in control of all, the One whose power and strength are unmatched, and pour out your heart. Tell him what you worry about, who you are concerned about, what you need his help with, and what you want him to do.

Never feel that your request is too small or too self-focused. If it's on your heart, God wants to know about it. You never need to feel that he doesn't want to listen to your prayers. God asks you to talk with him. He wants to hear, and he promises not only to listen but to answer! He may not always answer in the way you want him to, but that's because he sees a bigger picture of life than you do, and his goals for you are that you will have a stronger faith and a deeper trust in him.

Honestly talk to God. Tell him your fears, disappointments, and concerns, and believe that he is listening. Then look for his answers. He will show you great and wonderful things. He promises!

57

Getting Out of Your Comfort Zone

This is what the LORD Almighty said: "Administer true justice; show mercy and compassion to one another. Do not oppress the widow or the fatherless, the foreigner or the poor. Do not plot evil against each other."

ZECHARIAH 7:9–10

Some people are easy to care about. You like them, so you care if they are suffering with an illness or if they have a need for meals or financial help. There are some people you naturally want to help with things like yard work or transportation for appointments or errands. However, there are some people who are not easy to help. Perhaps they have different beliefs from yours, or they seem unapproachable, or you feel you don't have much in common with them.

Yet true justice is to show mercy and compassion to everyone, not just those like us. People who are different from you—those to whom it may be more of a stretch to show mercy and kindness—may be the ones who need it most. They may be the most alone and afraid. You can be the vehicle that brings God's love to them. Be courageous enough to care for those who take you outside your comfort zone. Ask God to open your eyes to those who need a kind word, a hot meal, a ride, or just a smile. Ask him to make you willing and ready to show his love to those who need it most. He will give you the courage as he gives you the opportunities.

58

Courage to Answer

> The LORD came and stood there, calling as at the other times, "Samuel! Samuel!"
> Then Samuel said, "Speak, for your servant is listening."
>
> 1 SAMUEL 3:10

Sometimes children are very choosy as to when they will respond to a parent's call. At times they choose to ignore the call until the parent's voice reaches a certain decibel level. Maybe they do this because they're afraid of being disciplined or given a chore to do. Whatever the reason, they may not answer until the situation is serious and by then, they could very well be in trouble.

What if Samuel had refused to answer God's call? What if, when God called "Samuel!" for the fourth time, the young boy had closed his eyes and pretended to be asleep? We might not be reading his story in the Bible then.

Well, what if God called your name? Would you have the courage to answer, "Speak, for your servant is listening"? Are you courageous enough to listen to what God has to say and then do what he asks you to do? Okay, maybe you won't hear God's audible voice, but he will speak to you through his Word. He will guide you, teach you, and challenge you. Will you listen? Will you answer? Will you respond?

59

Complete Trust

Trust in the Lord with all your heart
  and lean not on your own understanding;
in all your ways submit to him,
  and he will make your paths straight.

PROVERBS 3:5–6

Trusting God is a big part of building a relationship with him. Does it take courage to trust him? Yes, but even more than courage, trusting God is based on the understanding of how very much he loves you. Remember that God loves you so deeply that he sent his only Son to earth to teach about him and his love for you. Jesus then took the penalty for your sins on himself. He was tortured and killed to pay the price for your sins and make it possible for you to have a personal relationship with God. That was all done because of his love for you. You know that someone who loves you that much certainly wants only good things for you, which should make it easier for you to trust God.

Trusting God is very important, but don't miss two vital things in these verses from Proverbs. You read that you must trust God "with all your heart" and submit to him "in all your ways." You cannot trust God partway or submit only when you feel like it. Go all in with God and enjoy the blessings of his love and guidance.

60

Courage to Rejoice

Rejoice always, pray continually, give thanks in all circumstances; for this is God's will for you in Christ Jesus.
1 Thessalonians 5:16–18

Gratitude comes easily when things are going well in your life. However, even when we remember to thank God for his blessings in the good times, we may struggle with thanking him in the hard times.

It takes strength and courage to have an attitude of gratefulness when you're buried in pain and trouble—and yet God says to rejoice, no matter what's going on, and be thankful in every circumstance. Does he know how hard that is?

Of course he knows it's hard. It does take strength and courage to remain positive when you're hurting, but when you trust God and believe that he is in control, no

123

matter what is happening, you have the courage to rejoice in the hard times. You recognize that God is teaching you through the struggles you have and, in fact, they draw you closer to him. So even in hard times you can rejoice and be grateful!

61

Controlling Your Thought Life

Finally, brothers and sisters, whatever is true, whatever is noble, whatever is right, whatever is pure, whatever is lovely, whatever is admirable—if anything is excellent or praiseworthy—think about such things.

PHILIPPIANS 4:8

You know what happens when you have a big, beautiful basket of fruit that looks so very delicious, but buried in the middle of the basket is a piece of rotten fruit. If you don't take it out, it spreads its decay to any other fruit that's touching it. What began as one small bad spot can destroy much of the good fruit.

Your thought life can be that way. One small negative or critical thought can spread throughout your attitude if you do not courageously, intentionally pluck it out.

Intentionally pushing aside thoughts that do not honor God and others is done by replacing them with healthier thoughts. Focus your mind on the truth of Scripture. Fill your mind with the encouragement of God's love for you and the reminders of his patience and forgiveness.

Sometimes you may need God's help to see beyond the negativity of the present moment. Ask him to help you notice the evidence of his presence, protection, and love in each situation and in each person with whom you have contact. Remember his past work in your life to be reminded of his love in the present. Think on those things.

62

Growing in Godliness

Physical training is of some value, but godliness has value for all things, holding promise for both the present life and the life to come.

1 TIMOTHY 4:8

Learning to be godly means learning to think, feel, and behave more like God than like a person who doesn't know him at all. Does this happen easily? No, it doesn't. That's why it takes courage to commit to learning and growing toward godliness. The effort to grow more godly improves your life here on earth as well as the lives of those around you. Godliness goes even beyond your earthly life because as you live for God you also lay up treasures in heaven.

Think about how you strengthen and train your body's muscles. The only way to do so is by exercising them over and over to make them stronger. You have to be intentional, consistent, and persistent. You have to accept that your muscles will get tired and sore as they grow stronger.

Training for godliness also takes intentionality, consistency, and persistence. These characteristics are applied to the acts of studying God's Word each day, praying, and asking for his help. Growing closer to God often comes only through pain and suffering, so be ready! Realize that the privilege of knowing God and growing to be like him is worth whatever comes.

63

Courage to Praise

Let everything that has breath praise the Lord.
Praise the Lord.

PSALM 150:6

It shouldn't take courage to praise the Lord. But in a culture that's critical of God and anything related to him, you may sometimes need to summon courage for the simple act of praising God.

It's an interesting dilemma because praising God is a wonderful experience, so of course it's something you want to do. Praising God lifts your spirits and reminds you of the many blessings he showers on you. Praise reminds you of his power, strength, and love. God tells you to praise him. In fact, as this verse says, everything that breathes should praise the Lord.

Praising God with your words and attitudes tells other people how important he is to you. Your praise helps others learn about him and how strong, powerful, creative, and loving he is. Publicly praising God is a witness to others.

Praising God is also a witness to you because it helps you overcome discouragement and doubts. As you spend time mentioning his blessings, his gifts, and the times he has helped or protected you, you and others will see his love.

Ask God for the courage to openly praise him and to share your praise with anyone around you. Make praise your witness!

64

A New You

I will give you a new heart and put a new spirit in you; I will remove from you your heart of stone and give you a heart of flesh.

EZEKIEL 36:26

Who were you before you asked God into your life? If you were rebellious, dishonest, or not very nice, you may find it hard to forgive yourself for things you did or said. It's difficult to move forward in your new life if you're holding on to the old one out of guilt.

Here's the good news: no matter what kind of person you were before—rebellious, cynical, abusive, unkind—it doesn't matter. God will change you from the inside out by changing your heart. Your hardened heart, which keeps you at a distance from him, will be softened to be caring, considerate, compassionate, and loving. That's God's influence in your life. He sees the person you can be when he is in your life.

Don't give up on yourself. Believe that God can—and will—change your heart to help you become more like him. All you have to do is be willing to let him teach you, guide you, and give you that new spirit and caring heart.

65

Never Changing

Jesus Christ is the same yesterday and today and forever.

HEBREWS 13:8

In our world, things change at lightning speed. Technology is outdated as soon as you learn it. Friends may move away or fade from your life. Jobs disappear. Where can you put your confidence and trust?

There's only one Person and situation you can trust to never change, and that is Jesus and his love for you. You can always trust his love because many times in Scripture he promises his constant, unconditional, forgiving love. You can also trust that the standards and commandments of obedience to God that Jesus taught will never change. What was right hundreds of years ago is still right today. Jesus promised to always be with you, no matter what. Nothing can change that. Nothing can separate you from his incredible love.

Step courageously into your life in Jesus, knowing that you can depend on the fact that he is still the same Jesus you meet in Scripture. You can trust that he longs to know and forgive you and that he longs for your love for him and your faith in him to grow deeper.

66

In the Tough Times

I know what it is to be in need, and I know what it is to have plenty. I have learned the secret of being content in any and every situation, whether well fed or hungry, whether living in plenty or in want.

PHILIPPIANS 4:12

Praising God in the sunshine is easy. Praising God in the storm—not so much. When life is good, when everyone is healthy, when your job is successful—well, if you take time to actually think about it—of course you feel thankful and perhaps even verbalize your thanks to God.

Why does it take courage to praise God when life is hard, when you face health struggles, or when your job is taken away? Even beyond your own struggle to really praise God during these times, others may question what you have to praise God for or where your God is when you're struggling against so many negatives.

Praising in the hard times may be difficult, but that is when your trust in God is most obvious to yourself and others and when it is truly the most real. You can praise in the difficult times as well as the wonderful times because you know that God is always with you. Believe and trust that his love and strength will see you through whatever comes.

Praise God with courage and boldness, whatever your circumstance may be. Your praise becomes your testimony of his faithfulness.

67

No Fear

When I am afraid, I put my trust in you.
In God, whose word I praise—
in God I trust and am not afraid.
What can mere mortals do to me?

PSALM 56:3–4

Where do you turn when you're scared? Where do you find comfort? There can be some temptation to turn to food, money, friends, success, yourself, or a multitude of other things, when the only true solution to your fear is God.

Trust God. His Word proclaims his strength and power. Nothing and no one is greater than he is. Not others who judge or criticize you. Not your anxiety about your job and what your future might be. Not your fears about things that are happening in the world.

His Word also promises that there is nothing that can separate you from his love. That means you have no reason to fear any person or any situation. God's power, knowledge, and strength can take on anything you face. And he will take it on because he loves you even more than you can possibly imagine.

When you're afraid, spend time reading God's Word. It will remind you of God's presence, power, and love.

68

Work to Do

Have I not commanded you? Be strong and courageous. Do not be afraid; do not be discouraged, for the LORD your God will be with you wherever you go.

JOSHUA 1:9

God gives you opportunities to do different jobs for him throughout your lifetime. You may feel confident about doing some of the work. But some tasks may frighten you because they seem bigger than life, they're too difficult, they demand too much responsibility, or you feel untrained and unprepared for them.

It's okay that you have these anxious feelings as long as you don't stay there. When a job seems too difficult or a responsibility seems overwhelming, turn to God for help. He gave you the work to do, and he will make certain that you have what you need to accomplish it. Tell him you're overwhelmed or unprepared. Ask him for the knowledge, discernment, and skill to not only do the work but do it well.

Then enter into the job knowing that God is with you each step of the way. When you need knowledge, he will supply it or he will bring someone alongside you who can help you.

Be strong and courageous because your God has work for you, and he will make sure you are prepared to do it. Lean on him. Listen to him. Trust him.

69

Nothing in Return

God demonstrates his own love for us in this: While we were still sinners, Christ died for us.

ROMANS 5:8

What does it take for you to forgive someone who has hurt you? Is it necessary for them to repent and apologize for their behavior? Can you forgive them even if they give no indication that they are sorry for hurting you?

It is hard to forgive when you've been hurt, especially when it's by the actions of someone you love. But your example to follow is Jesus himself. He paid the ultimate price of giving his own life as the sacrifice to pay for your sins. He did that regardless of whether you would ever acknowledge or be sorry for your sin. He sacrificed because of his depth of love for you. He didn't demand anything from you before he did this. His love was enough.

Refusing to forgive another person until you get what you feel you deserve is a very human emotion. However, the goal in following Christ is to learn from his example. Be willing to let go of what you think you deserve and simply love and forgive without expecting anything in return. You will make your own heart healthier, and you will be showing a true example of God's love.

70

On Guard

Be on your guard; stand firm in the faith; be courageous; be strong. Do everything in love.

1 CORINTHIANS 16:13–14

Maybe you know this feeling: Something doesn't seem right, and you start feeling nervous, on edge. Your skin even feels prickly. Every sound reverberates in your mind. Every movement catches your eye. You are on guard because something is going to happen and you are prepared to face it.

Scripture tells you to be on guard where your faith is concerned. Pay attention to the temptations that try to pull you away from closeness with God. There will be times when Satan tries to direct you into focusing on yourself or having a critical spirit or, well, any of a myriad of behaviors that are disobedient to God's commands. Satan works so subtly that you may not realize your behavior is changing.

That's why you must be on guard. Stay in the Word. Listen to the Spirit's promptings in your heart. Be courageous and strong in asking Jesus to help you fight temptation. Know that God loves you very much and he will be your strength and help. Stand strong in your faith because of your love for him.

71

Courage to Honor God

Whether you eat or drink or whatever you do, do it all for the glory of God.

1 Corinthians 10:31

There's a wonderful illustration of this verse in the first chapter of the book of Daniel. Young Daniel and his friends were captives being trained to serve in the king's palace. They were strong, intelligent fellows who caught the eye of the official in charge. He put them in a special training program to serve the king. That meant they got better treatment and better food than the other captives. You might think that Daniel would be a fool to give up this elevated position, that he would be foolish to risk offending the official or the king. But he did.

Daniel knew that the food he and his friends were served had first been offered to idols. Because Daniel loved and served God, he believed it was wrong to eat it. So he courageously made a deal with the official. He and his friends

Courage to Honor God

were given only vegetables and water for ten days while the other young men ate the king's food. If he and his friends weren't the strongest and healthiest of all after the ten days, then they would eat the king's food. God honored Daniel's courage, and he and his friends were the strongest of all!

Is there a stand you should take to show that your faith in God and your desire to honor him are the most important things to you? Do you have the courage to take that stand? God will honor your bravery.

72

The Only Salvation

Salvation is found in no one else, for there is no other name under heaven given to mankind by which we must be saved.

ACTS 4:12

Daniel 3 tells the story of three young men who believed that their salvation came from God and who chose to honor him. King Nebuchadnezzar commanded everyone to bow down to a gold statue he had made, but Shadrach, Meshach, and Abednego refused, declaring that they bowed only before God. The king wasn't happy about that. He offered them another chance to obey, and their refusal would mean they would be tossed into a blazing furnace. These three God followers didn't hesitate; again they declared they would bow only to God. They believed God would protect them if they went into the furnace.

What did Shadrach, Meshach, and Abednego expect to happen? Would God pour water in the furnace to put out the fire? Would he change the king's mind? Would he whisk them away?

God didn't do any of those things. The boys were tossed into a furnace so hot that the soldiers who threw them in were killed. But God honored their faith. An angel of God came into the furnace with them. They weren't burned— they didn't even smell like smoke when the amazed king called them out.

Shadrach, Meshach, and Abednego had the courage to face the fire, and God honored that faith. Do you need to choose to trust God rather than follow someone who wants you to turn away from him? Be courageous enough to honor God, and then be amazed at how he honors you.

73

Courage When Things Look Hopeless

He is the living God
and he endures forever;
his kingdom will not be destroyed,
his dominion will never end.
He rescues and he saves;
he performs signs and wonders
in the heavens and on the earth.
He has rescued Daniel
from the power of the lions.

DANIEL 6:26–27

When you diligently obey God and stand up for him, do you expect him to protect you from problems? Consider Daniel. He loved and obeyed God. He took a stand of obedience to God early in his life and continued it throughout his life. Daniel valued his prayer life—his personal communication with God. So even when his enemies got the king to decree that no one could pray to anyone but him, Daniel continued praying to God, and he didn't try to hide it.

Daniel's choice to honor God resulted in his being tossed into a den of lions. God didn't protect Daniel from the prescribed punishment; however, God did protect Daniel from the lions. He honored Daniel's obedience, just not in the way Daniel may have expected.

Do you have the courage to honor God, even when you face persecution, whether it comes through sarcasm, humiliation, or physical danger? Do you trust God to protect you because of your obedience? Are you willing to accept the form his protection takes, even if it isn't what you hoped for? He does know what's happening, and he loves you and has a plan. Trust him.

74

Brave Changes

Don't urge me to leave you or to turn back from you. Where you go I will go, and where you stay I will stay. Your people will be my people and your God my God.

RUTH 1:16

When life as you know it seems to fall apart, do you have the courage to start over? God may turn your life in a completely new direction, which could draw you closer to him—but it could also be frightening. It could mean leaving everything that's familiar behind.

Consider Ruth. It seemed that her life was set—be a wife, have a family, grow old. Then her husband died, and everything changed. She could have gone home to her parents, but Ruth had seen something in the life of her mother-in-law, Naomi, that she was drawn to—Naomi's faith in God. When Naomi decided to return to her homeland, Ruth chose to go with her. She left behind everything that was familiar, including the faith of her childhood and family. The way her mother-in-law lived her life attracted Ruth to God, and she wanted him in her life. Ruth had the courage to make a change, and that courage gave her a new life and a new faith.

Life changes are stressful. It's difficult to adjust to new places and situations. Having the courage to follow when God leads you to new things offers growth in your faith and ministry for him. Be courageous and experience new things!

75

According to His Will

> *This is the confidence we have in approaching God: that if we ask anything according to his will, he hears us.*
>
> 1 JOHN 5:14

Have you ever so desperately wanted God to do something for you that you literally cried out to him, begging him for action? Crying out is not a subdued, silent prayer but a tear-filled, passionate, breathless cry for his attention, care, and work.

Hannah did that. In 1 Samuel, chapter 1, we read that Hannah wanted more than anything to have a baby. She wanted a child so desperately that she fell to the ground and cried out to God for the blessing of motherhood. She cried aloud, not caring who heard her.

Sometimes we box prayers in by feeling that they need to be quiet and humble in order for us to show how much trust and submission are behind them. Some feel that if they cry out with passion, it may appear that they aren't happy with what God is doing.

It's okay to cry out to God with passion. Tell him what you want! Your cries do not mean you don't trust him or that you won't accept it if he does something different. He wants to know the passion in your heart. You can verbalize it to him. Then ask for the strength to accept whatever comes. As Jesus prayed: "Not my will, but yours" (Luke 22:42).

76

Brown Sugar Giving

Give, and it will be given to you. A good measure, pressed down, shaken together and running over, will be poured into your lap. For with the measure you use, it will be measured to you.

LUKE 6:38

Who doesn't love a freshly baked chocolate chip cookie? Warm, right from the oven, with soft, gooey chocolate chips—yum! If you are a baker, you know that a necessary ingredient in these sweet treats is brown sugar. Measuring brown sugar for your recipe is different from measuring other ingredients. Brown sugar is measured by packing it down into the measuring cup and pressing it firmly, so it seems that you're putting in twice as much as the recipe calls for.

Think about that kind of measurement as you consider giving, sharing, and encouraging and loving others. Step out of your comfort zone if necessary, and give until you think you can't give anymore. Give until it's obvious to all that your love for others is overflowing. Give of your time, energy, funds, and talents from the generosity of your heart. Even if no one gives you a pat on the back and you feel like no one notices, you can be sure that God notices. He sees the brown sugar sacrificial giving flowing from your heart, and you will be blessed for it.

77

Trusting God to Provide

Do not worry, saying, "What shall we eat?" or "What shall we drink?" or "What shall we wear?" For the pagans run after all these things, and your heavenly Father knows that you need them.

MATTHEW 6:31–32

Believing God will provide in a situation that appears to be hopeless is courageous faith. The widow who is described in 2 Kings 4 was in a desperate situation. After her husband's death, his creditor came after her. She had no money, so the man threatened to take her sons as slaves to pay the debt. When she asked Elisha for help, he asked what she had in the house. All she had was a jar of oil. He told her to send her sons to gather pots from the neighbors and fill them with the oil. She did, and the jar of oil did not run out until the last pot was filled. What an amazing story! We don't know for certain if the woman sold the oil as Elisha told her to do. But we can assume she obeyed the man of God and sold the oil to pay the creditor.

If so, she was saved from a hopeless situation. Where is the courage in her story? She did what Elisha—a man of God—told her to do, even though it could have made her look foolish to her sons and her neighbors.

No situation is hopeless when God is involved. Pull from the depth of your faith to trust him to work through whatever you're facing, and wait in strength and courage to see how he will save you.

78

Waiting for God's Timing

Be patient, then, brothers and sisters, until the Lord's coming.
See how the farmer waits for the land to yield its valuable crop,
patiently waiting for the autumn and spring rains.

Life brings various seasons as relationships, health, careers, and situations ebb and flow. Some things are wonderful, joy-filled blessings. Some are difficult and painful. It's important to have the courage to be patient during all seasons of life, and the comparison to nature in this verse reminds us of that. When a seed is planted in the ground, a plant does not immediately pop up. There are no flowers, no tomatoes on the vine, right away. The farmer must wait for the seed to respond to water, nutrients in the soil, and sunlight. Farming takes patience.

When the seasons of life bring difficult times, have the courage to wait. See how God grows your faith and teaches you to trust more deeply in him through the ways he brings water, nutrients, and sunlight into your situation. You will see that your courageous patience is rewarded in your walk with God, just as the farmer's patience is rewarded with the long anticipated crop. Good things come, even from hard times and even when we must wait.

79

It's Not Over

*If we confess our sins, he is faithful and just and will forgive us
our sins and purify us from all unrighteousness.*

1 JOHN 1:9

God graciously forgives our failures when we ask because
he sees whether our heart truly desires to obey him.

The book of 2 Samuel tells of King David's affair with
Bathsheba, who was another man's wife. Bathsheba became
pregnant as a result of the affair. David tried to cover up the
affair by bringing her husband home from the war, assuming
husband and wife would sleep together. When that didn't
happen, he had the man sent to the front lines of the war so
he would be killed. David put a lot of work into covering up
the first sin in this domino effect, yet God still referred to
David as a man after God's own heart. Why? What did God
see that no one else saw?

God saw deep into David's heart, which showed that even
though he sinned and made bad choices, David was sorry for

what he had done. He loved God and God's Word, he was repentant, and he was thankful for the renewal of forgiveness and second chances. David made the most of his second chance by honoring and praising God.

Maybe you've messed up big-time in your life. Maybe you feel that what you've done is unforgivable and that you are now damaged goods, so you could never serve God. That's not true. Believe in God's forgiveness and in the second chances he gladly gives. Maybe your story was changed by your sin and bad choices, but it isn't hopeless. Learn from David—your story is not over. God forgives. He looks at your heart.

80

Eternally Alive

Jesus said to her, "I am the resurrection and the life. The one who believes in me will live, even though they die; and whoever lives by believing in me will never die. Do you believe this?"

JOHN 11:25–26

When Lazarus, the brother of Mary and Martha, died, the faith of his sisters was put to the test. Jesus was their good friend. They knew he could heal their brother, so they sent for him, but he didn't come until it was too late. When he arrived, Martha said, "Lord, . . . if you had been here, my brother would not have died" (John 11:21). It almost sounds like she blamed him for her brother's death because he didn't hurry to their sides.

Jesus's response to Martha was simply that she should believe. He is the resurrection and the life. He promises that all who believe in him will never die. Martha just needed to believe. You may know the rest of the story: Jesus called Lazarus from the grave back to life—for a while, at least.

Do you have the courage to believe when your heart is breaking from the loss of a loved one? Will Jesus call your loved one back to earthly life? Probably not. But he promised eternal life to those who have accepted him as their Savior, so when they close their eyes on earth, they open their eyes in heaven. Forever alive with Jesus. He promised.

81

Jumping Out of the Boat

I can do all this through him who gives me strength.
PHILIPPIANS 4:13

Peter . . . impetuous, passionate risk taker. When Peter believed something, he was in 100 percent, and he didn't much care what anyone else thought. He believed Jesus's love, power, and strength were his, so when he saw Jesus walking toward the disciples' boat one day—on top of the water—he called out, "If it's you, . . . tell me to come to you on the water" (Matt. 14:28). Jesus told him to come, so Peter leaped out of the boat and started walking toward Jesus—ON TOP of the water! That was Peter. When he wanted something, he had the courage to go for it. When his focus on Jesus wavered, he sank. But Jesus saved him!

How's your courage? You may know the old saying, "If you keep on doing what you do, you'll keep on getting what you've got." If you want something new and exciting in your life, you must be willing to "get out of the boat." It can be pretty frightening, but you will never know the possibilities if you don't take the risk. Having the courage to take a chance opens the door for Jesus to show you new pathways in your life.

82

The Power of Change

The LORD is my strength and my shield;
my heart trusts in him, and he helps me.

PSALM 28:7

All the believers knew about Saul. Acts 8:3 reads, "Saul began to destroy the church. Going from house to house, he dragged off both men and women and put them in prison." Saul was known for persecuting believers. Christians were scared of him, so when God told Ananias, "Go to the house of Judas on Straight Street and ask for a man from Tarsus named Saul, for he is praying" (Acts 9:11), Ananias questioned the wisdom of that command. That's understandable because Ananias didn't yet know that Saul had met Jesus and was a changed man. But, to Ananias's credit, when God said, "Go," he went. He courageously trusted that Saul could change from the dangerous man he had been to a servant of God.

Do you believe that people can change 100 percent once Jesus comes into their hearts? If God told you to spend some time with someone who had been very far away from him and whose lifestyle and morals were completely the opposite of yours, would you have the courage to obey?

God can save anyone and completely rehab a heart that has been against him. If God gives you the opportunity to be a part of someone's new life for him, as he did with Ananias and Saul, be courageous and take the chance!

Courage to Obey

This is how we know that we love the children of God: by loving God and carrying out his commands.

1 JOHN 5:2

There may be times when God asks you to do something that makes absolutely no sense to you. That's what happened to Noah when God told him to build a boat . . . a very big boat. There was no reason for Noah to build a boat that big when no large body of water was close by. His friends thought he was a little crazy when he started working on it, but Noah obeyed God no matter what.

Noah had the courage to do what God asked, even when he saw no reason for it and he had to endure the comments of friends.

God does not always tell you the *why* of what he asks of you or the reason for circumstances that come into your life.

He asks you to trust him completely and to have the courage to obey and follow him, even when you can't see the *why*. Are you willing to step into darkness, trusting that your foot will land on something solid, even when you can't see it? Put your faith into courageous action.

84

Greatest Faith

When Jesus heard this, he was amazed at him, and turning to the crowd following him, he said, "I tell you, I have not found such great faith even in Israel."

LUKE 7:9

How would you like to be the person Jesus referred to when he said he had never found such great faith before? It would be quite an honor, wouldn't it? The military officer to whom Jesus was referring had a servant whom he really cared about—the man was either a good servant or had become a friend. When the servant became very ill, the officer knew that Jesus could help. What's so amazing about this man's faith was that he believed Jesus could heal his servant without even coming to him. He knew that all Jesus needed to do was speak words of healing. The officer didn't have to be with his servant and see the healing in order to know it happened. He trusted Jesus that much.

Faith that doesn't have to see is courageous. Having faith that deep means that you believe God is working and answering your prayers. That you trust his timing and his choices in regard to what is best for all involved. It's not easy to always be courageous, but it's something to aspire to. Trust God so completely and be so convinced of his love that you believe in his answers before they are actually seen.

85

Courage to Face My Sin

I do not do the good I want to do, but the evil I do not want to do—this I keep on doing. Now if I do what I do not want to do, it is no longer I who do it, but it is sin living in me that does it.

ROMANS 7:19–20

Wouldn't it be nice if you could rewind life an hour or so at a time so you could do a little better? You know, respond with more kindness to a situation, be a bit more patient, listen more than talk, be generous without resentment . . . there are a multitude of things you might want to change if you got a do-over.

The easy way out is to blame your less-than-perfect behavior on someone or something else. But while someone or something else may have played into your words and actions, the bottom-line reason for them is sin. When sin has a foothold in your heart, it controls what you do, even when you don't really want to do it.

Be courageous—admit that you *do* sin instead of blaming other factors for your behavior. Ask the Lord to help you overcome sin in your life so you can grow to be more like Jesus. Remember that the Christian life is a journey and that you're always learning and growing.

86

Courage to Be You

We are God's handiwork, created in Christ Jesus to do good works, which God prepared in advance for us to do.

EPHESIANS 2:10

Self-esteem is an interesting topic to think about. You don't want to have so much self-esteem that it becomes pride, which leaves God out of consideration, but you should have enough self-esteem to be confident in who God made you to be.

This verse from Ephesians says that we are God's handiwork. Other Bible versions call us his masterpiece—the best of his work. Each person is created with unique talents, gifts, and personalities. In other words, God made you exactly the way he wants you to be. He doesn't want you to get stuck in the trap of comparing yourself to another person, wondering if you should be more like them. He wants you to be you. In fact, he doesn't just *want* you to be you, he *needs* you to be you. When each person is being who he made them to be and doing what he made them to do, all the parts of his kingdom fit together like a well-oiled machine.

Don't get caught in the trap of feeling you must be who the world says you should be. Have the courage to push aside what others think, and believe that you are special because of who God says you are and because of the way he made you.

87

Courage That Makes You Creative

By this everyone will know that you are my disciples, if you love one another.

JOHN 13:35

What a blessing friendship is. Sharing life with good friends makes life so much better. Are you the kind of person who would go out of your way to help your friends?

The men in Luke 5 went out of their way to help a sick friend. They got creative in order to bring the paralyzed man to Jesus and ask for healing for him. They carried their friend to the house where Jesus was teaching, but they couldn't get through the crowd of people there. That's when they got creative and took a chance. They tore a hole in the roof of the house and lowered the man down in front of Jesus. Would Jesus chastise them for disrupting his teaching? Would the homeowner be upset that they made a hole in the roof?

Would others who were waiting for Jesus's attention be upset that these men pushed their way ahead of them? The men didn't care. They were courageously creative in order to help their friend.

The only response to their actions that we know of is that of Jesus. He saw their faith as well as the sick man's faith, and he healed the man.

Are you courageously creative when it comes to helping others? Will you go out of your way to do so? Are you willing to be inconvenienced? Are you willing to be the kind of friend that you would like to have?

88

Greatest Commandments

"Love the Lord your God with all your heart and with all your soul and with all your strength and with all your mind"; and, "Love your neighbor as yourself."

LUKE 10:27

The hard part of obeying these two greatest commandments that Jesus gave is getting yourself out of the way. This verse challenges you to love God more than anything or anyone else—even yourself. Loving God as fully as this verse describes means completely trusting him with your life and willingly submitting your desires to him. It means giving all your thoughts, actions, and emotions over to him, and believing that what he chooses to bring into your life is all for your good. Understand that even if painful struggles come, they provide the opportunity to trust God more deeply and to grow closer to him.

The second commandment given here is to love your neighbor as yourself. What does that mean to you? It's actually more than what you may think at first. Loving another as you love yourself is actually loving another *more* than you love yourself. It's difficult to have the best interests of two people at the forefront of your mind. Putting others above yourself may not be easy, but doing so will show Jesus's love to others and draw you closer to God.

89

Guard Your Heart

Above all else, guard your heart,
for everything you do flows from it.

PROVERBS 4:23

Sin is sneaky. Satan is subtle. Each can slip into your life in such tiny ways that you may not even notice the changes in your actions and attitudes. It may happen so gradually that the sinful things slowly become habits that you're comfortable with, so they don't feel like sin.

Why does this Bible verse tell you to guard your heart? Possibly because sin often begins with a yearning, something you want to have or do. It may also start with the feeling that you deserve something or have been wronged in some way. If your heart isn't submitted to God and focused on obeying, serving, and reflecting him to others, those negative feelings will take root and grow into full-fledged sin.

How do you guard your heart? It's best to do so by asking God to hold you accountable for your thoughts and feelings. Ask him to reveal the beginning of sinful thoughts that might be running through your heart, and then ask him to give you the courage and strength to push them aside before they take root.

90

A Step at a Time

*If my people, who are called by my name, will humble them-
selves and pray and seek my face and turn from their wicked
ways, then I will hear from heaven, and I will forgive their sin
and will heal their land.*

2 Chronicles 7:14

What does this verse say to you? What do you hear God
asking of his people? He's asking you to allow him to
be the most important Person in your life. He's asking you to
submit to him by giving up control of your life and following him. Is this scary? Well, it could be if you don't honestly
trust that God loves you intensely and unconditionally and
therefore has your best interests in mind.

To get to the point of trusting God in your relationship
with him, you must get yourself out of the way. Stop trying
to control your life. Submit to God's plan. Follow him even
if you can't see the end result of his plan yet. Learn that you

can trust him because he sees the big picture of your entire life and the role you play in his work on this earth.

Your courage may come one step at a time by trusting God in a small instance and, after seeing his love and care for you, knowing you can trust him in something bigger. Give yourself permission to grow in courage and trust, a step at a time, and learn to fully submit to him.

words of
hope
for
Women

1

Hope of Heaven

Praise be to the God and Father of our Lord Jesus Christ! In his great mercy he has given us new birth into a living hope through the resurrection of Jesus Christ from the dead, and into an inheritance that can never perish, spoil or fade. This inheritance is kept in heaven for you, who through faith are shielded by God's power until the coming of the salvation that is ready to be revealed in the last time.

1 PETER 1:3–5

How amazing is it that you have the hope of eternal life in heaven with Jesus? That hope for heaven doesn't mean it might or might not happen. Forever in heaven is a certainty if you have accepted Jesus as your Savior, because God raised Jesus from the dead. You're part of their family now. The promise of eternity is true, and it will never change. Heaven will be wonderful—forever! To be in God's presence in the beautiful glory of heaven, reunited with loved ones— what a glorious hope!

Another part of God's promise of hope is that he is keeping watch over you until you are promoted to the glory of heaven. Once you've been adopted into his family by your acceptance of Jesus, God promises you a place in his heaven forever. But you're not free-floating between now and then. God's power and love are watching over you. You don't ever have to be afraid of what life brings. You can call out to him for help whenever you need it. He's ready to fight for you!

2

Hope Comes from Trust

God remembered Noah and all the wild animals and the livestock that were with him in the ark, and he sent a wind over the earth, and the waters receded.

GENESIS 8:1

God saved Noah from the flood that wiped out civilization as it was. He put Noah and his family on the ark where they rode out the storm. It must have been frightening. Did they hear the cries of those who died? Were the animals skittish with fear as the ark bounced around in the storm? Did it feel like they were on the ark forever? It had been 150 days. Did Noah have any communication from God in that time? Did he wonder if God remembered them? Noah had hope for the "what's next" in his life because God had assured him he would save him from the flood. He had hope because he trusted God.

How's your hope level these days? Do you trust God to remember what you're going through? Do you trust that his plan to rescue you or help you will actually come to fruition? Without trust there is no hope. Without relationship there is no trust. God did rescue Noah in his time and with his preordained plan. He will also rescue you in his time and with his plan. Keep your hope level high as you trust the One who promises to help you.

3

True Joy

May the God of hope fill you with all joy and peace as you trust in him, so that you may overflow with hope by the power of the Holy Spirit.

ROMANS 15:13

How do you define joy? What does it look like in your life? Joy is different from happiness, which is a fleeting emotion. Happiness is great, but it comes from experiences you have or interactions with people you enjoy. It comes and goes.

Joy comes from deep within your heart. It is not dependent on external circumstances. In fact, you can have joy even when your circumstances are unpleasant. That's because true joy comes from trusting God and knowing his love and care in your life. Your relationship with him is the source of joy because you have the power of his Holy Spirit available to give you strength to fight off temptations that compromise your decision to live for him. When you trust that the situations in your life are God's will for you, you know that the unpleasantness or unhappiness is only for the moment. Joy comes from your hope in God's good plan for you.

4

Hope in Fighting Temptation

No temptation has overtaken you except what is common to mankind. And God is faithful; he will not let you be tempted beyond what you can bear. But when you are tempted, he will also provide a way out so that you can endure it.

1 CORINTHIANS 10:13

Temptation is hard to resist. It's . . . tempting. Whether you're fighting the temptation to eat one more chocolate chip cookie or to sleep in instead of getting up to exercise, it's hard. Some temptation goes deeper, like cheating on your taxes, cheating on your spouse, joining in a judgmental, critical assessment of another person . . . anything that takes you away from showing God's love to others by your obedience to him.

Satan throws temptation at you many times every day. Sometimes it's subtle, sometimes more obvious, but he is persistent because he knows constant temptation wears you down until you give in. His goal is to pull you away from God and make you believe you have failed him.

But even if you sometimes give in to temptation, it doesn't mean you've failed God! He loves you and will forgive you. You have the hope of victory because you have God! Cry out to him. Scream if you need to. Ask for his strength and power to help you withstand the temptation. God may not take the temptation away, but his strength will help you resist it and stay true to your faith in him.

5

Hope in God's Comfort

He heals the brokenhearted
and binds up their wounds.
PSALM 147:3

Perhaps you know someone who has suffered a broken heart. Heartbreak can be debilitating. A person who is grieving may be so lost in her grief that she withdraws from life. Staying home, not engaging with others, not eating . . . or eating too much. Maybe she can see no way out of the grief and no life beyond it. Getting through grief seems pretty hopeless for her. Maybe that someone is you . . . or has been at some point in your life.

You can find hope for restoration in trusting that God will help you pick up the pieces of your broken heart and make sense of life again. He will heal your wounds and help you through the pain of grief. God loves you, and while loss of relationships and physical death are a part of life, he will give you the strength to get through the pain. His comfort will give you a new lease on life. It may take time, but eventually you will begin to notice the sunshine again. You will join back into life with your family and friends.

Keep hoping in God's comfort and love. You won't be disappointed.

6

Ask and You Shall Receive

Ask and it will be given to you; seek and you will find; knock and the door will be opened to you. For everyone who asks receives; the one who seeks finds; and to the one who knocks, the door will be opened.

MATTHEW 7:7–8

If you're a control freak, these might be your dream verses. They sort of make it sound like you can ask God for anything you want and—*boom*—it's yours. Wouldn't that be quite a deal? Maybe, but it isn't what these verses promise. They actually promise something better. They offer the opportunity for you to let go. Stop trying to control your life; let go and let God control it.

These verses are promised to those who are walking closely with Christ. People who spend time each day reading and absorbing God's Word. People who are so submitted to God that his desires become their desires for their lives. Now these verses make sense. You can ask anything of God because your heart and mind are seeking to honor and serve him. He will help you more fully understand his Word and grasp his leading. Ask God to open your heart and mind to him. You have the promised hope of answered prayer.

7

Promised Refuge

God is our refuge and strength,
an ever-present help in trouble.

PSALM 46:1

Imagine you've gone out for an evening walk. The sky is cloudy but there's no rain. You walk for quite a while, enjoying the scenery. Then when you are a good distance from home, a sudden, violent storm blows up. Strong winds fling the trees around, rain pelts you, lightning streaks across the sky. It's scary! You need a safe place to hide from the storm. You need a refuge.

As storms blow up in your life (and they will), you will certainly hope for a refuge, a place where you can be safe from the danger of the storms. You do have the certain hope of a refuge in God. He is your safe place to hide from the storms of life. While you're tucked safely away, he will refresh your strength so that when you must face those storms again, you'll be strong enough to be ready.

The beauty of his promised refuge and strength is that he is always available. He's always ready to help you. In fact, he's waiting for you to call out to him. Your hope for refuge and strength has been fulfilled!

8

Hope in What Jesus Says

That day when evening came, he said to his disciples, "Let us go over to the other side."

MARK 4:35

Jesus spent the day teaching. In the evening, he and his disciples got into a boat, and Jesus said, "Let us go over to the other side." It was a simple suggestion and probably not one his friends thought much about. But after they got out on the lake, a sudden storm blew in. It was strong and the disciples were scared. But Jesus was sleeping. How could he sleep when they might die? You know the story—they woke him, he calmed the storm, then he asked why they had such little faith. Here's the thing . . . he said, "Let us go over to the other side." He didn't say, "Let's go halfway, then drown." The disciples didn't believe he meant what he said.

Do you believe Jesus will take care of you, guide you, and teach you? Do you believe what Scripture tells you about him, or do you question everything that happens to you? Do you only hope that he means what he says? Do you trust him to follow through and deliver you safely to the other side of whatever you're dealing with? Trust your hope in Jesus.

9

Jesus Cares

Jesus said to him, "Receive your sight; your faith has healed you." Immediately he received his sight and followed Jesus, praising God. When all the people saw it, they also praised God.

LUKE 18:42–43

Jesus was on his way to Jericho. He was surrounded by people as usual. They followed him everywhere, some to see what he would do and some to benefit from his miracle power. It must have been a little chaotic around him as he walked down the road. In the noise of that moment a single voice cried out, "Jesus, have mercy on me!" (see v. 38). A blind man told Jesus that he wanted to see. With all the people pressing in around him, wanting things from him, Jesus heard that one voice . . . and he answered. He gave the blind man sight.

Jesus cares about any problem you have too. You can be certain in the hope that whatever you're dealing with, he cares, and he can handle it. Don't believe the lie that your problem is too insignificant for God to pay attention to. Don't believe the lie that you have disappointed him too often for him to help you this time. It's not true. You can be secure in the hope that he cares and he will help you get through whatever you're facing today.

10

Hope for the Future

"I know the plans I have for you," declares the LORD, "plans to prosper you and not to harm you, plans to give you hope and a future."

JEREMIAH 29:11

Did you have your life all planned out? You expected to do this thing by that date and that thing by the next date and on and on. But life doesn't always go by your plan, does it? You may not have been too far into your plan when things started shifting and changing. How did you handle those changes? Does your future look uncertain now? Would you still like to have things planned out so you know what to expect?

When situations and people start changing in your life, the future can look pretty confusing to you. But even if things look mysterious now, you can know that your future is all planned—by God. He may reveal it to you only one step at a time, but if you trust him, your hope can rest assured in his plan.

God's plans for you are always good, though they may not always be easy. If you're struggling with something right now, know that his plans include times of teaching you and growing you to become more like Jesus. Those lessons are learned through difficult times. Trust what he's doing in your life, and know that it is all for your good.

11

Hope for Better Times

I have told you these things, so that in me you may have peace. In this world you will have trouble. But take heart! I have overcome the world.

JOHN 16:33

If you're a parent, you know that peace is a fleeting thing because a parent is often only as happy as her unhappiest child. If you're a citizen of the world—okay, that's everyone—then you know that peace in the world around you is an increasingly fleeting thing. It seems that people are more and more angry about more and more things. Peace between countries, people groups, families, and friends is very fragile. In these chaotic times, is there any hope of peace?

Jesus warned his followers that life was going to get messy for them, and it did. It gets messy for you too. Broken relationships, health challenges, rebellious children—peace is hard to come by.

But Jesus doesn't leave you hopeless. You can have the hope of peace by putting your faith in him. He is in control and yes, life gets messy, but nothing surprises him. He is teaching you through the hard times to lean on him. That understanding can help you have peace for this day and, of course, you have the hope of heaven where peace will reign forever.

12

Hope for the Helpless

You, LORD, hear the desire of the afflicted;
*   you encourage them, and you listen to their cry.*

PSALM 10:17

There are places around the world that seem to constantly be in a state of turmoil because of war, drought, storms, or poverty. Your heart must break for those people and the constant struggles they have to endure. It seems like they never have a chance to catch their breath or to have some peace and comfort in their world. It's hard to see where God might be in all of that.

There's no easy answer as to why God doesn't stop the wars or end the poverty or provide food and water. Why doesn't he help those people who are so afflicted? But you know that God is love, and his compassionate heart does care about them. The hope is that the people in those dire situations have comfort and peace in their hearts because they know that God has heard their cries.

The challenge is for Christians in more comfortable situations to reach out and help those in war-torn countries and poverty-stricken areas. Perhaps their help and hope is to come through God using your efforts.

13

Hope of Forgiveness

If we confess our sins, he is faithful and just and will forgive us our sins and purify us from all unrighteousness.

1 John 1:9

"I'm sorry. I'm so sorry. Please forgive me." When you want forgiveness from someone, you hope with all your heart that they will forgive your indiscretion and forget that it ever happened. That's the hope. But when someone asks your forgiveness, are you willing to forgive *and* forget? It's hard to forgive when you've been hurt, cheated, or lied to, isn't it?

That makes it even more amazing that when you ask God's forgiveness, he gives it, and not only does he forgive, he wipes away the memory of your sin. It's gone. There's no danger that he's keeping a list of your sins to bring up down the road somewhere. He isn't keeping a tally sheet to hit you with later. Whatever you have done, however you have sinned, no matter how many times or how often, God forgives you. Jesus paid the price for your sin, so when you confess your sin and ask his forgiveness, you get it! God promises his faithful forgiveness and cleansing for the rest of your life—all because he loves you. What a gift!

14

Hope for Growth

We boast in the hope of the glory of God. Not only so, but we also glory in our sufferings, because we know that suffering produces perseverance; perseverance, character; and character, hope.

ROMANS 5:2–4

What's the goal of exercise? It's to make you physically fit and therefore healthier, right? But exercise can be tiring and cause some pain. However, it's worth it in the long run because you get stronger, your balance is better, and your heart is healthier. You have to put in the work to get the benefit.

Spiritual growth also takes effort; some you can plan for, and some you cannot. Growing closer to God is something you want. Learning to trust him more—to trust his heart, to trust his plan—most often comes through difficulties in your life. When you're suffering or struggling and all you can do is hold on to him with all your strength, you learn.

The reward of holding on to God teaches you perseverance. Learning to keep on keeping on in your faith develops your character, which helps you become more like Christ in humility before God and dependence on him. This "spiritual workout" grows your faith-walk to make you more mature in Christ, and that's what God wants for you. Don't fight the process; instead, have hope in the outcome.

15

Hope for Guidance

Your word is a lamp for my feet,
a light on my path.
PSALM 119:105

Darkness so thick that you can't see your own hand in front of your face is pretty intense. Trying to make your way through such complete darkness is treacherous. You can trip over things, walk into things, and get completely disoriented so that you even go the wrong way.

Just a tiny little light in that complete darkness will shine like a beacon. It stands out brightly and gives you something to walk toward. It only takes a little bit of light to illuminate the darkness.

As you make your way through the chaos of life, do you sometimes feel that you're walking in total darkness? Do you long for some guidance and direction, some light in your world? God's Word will give you that. It becomes a light in your dark world, illuminating the path you should travel.

As you read God's Word and open your heart to its message and guidance, instructions for living in obedience to God become clearer. God's Word addresses how to obey him and how to treat other people. It lights your way and turns your heart toward obedience to God.

16

Hope in Your Advocate

*I will ask the Father, and he will give you another advocate
to help you and be with you forever—the Spirit of truth.
The world cannot accept him, because it neither sees him nor
knows him. But you know him, for he lives with you and will
be in you.*

JOHN 14:16–17

When you, as a law-abiding citizen, have to plead your
case to a police officer or worse, before a judge, it's
scary. You might get so nervous that you can't say the words
you need to speak to explain yourself or defend yourself.
Even if you're innocent you start to get short of breath, and
perspiration rolls down your forehead. What you need is an
advocate—someone who can speak for you and make sense
of the situation.

God knew you were going to need an advocate in all of life,
so he gave you one—his Holy Spirit. Because of his Spirit you

have the hope, or certainty, of being heard and understood. The Holy Spirit pleads your case as necessary. He speaks to God on your behalf. He prays the prayers that are about things so intense you can't find words to pray about them. He resides in your heart and guides your understanding of Scripture. He maneuvers you through decisions and choices when you may not be sure what is right for you. The Holy Spirit is God's gift to you, and he offers all you need to learn about living for God and obeying him.

17

Hope for Knowledge

Call to me and I will answer you and tell you great and un-searchable things you do not know.

JEREMIAH 33:3

Clueless people sometimes act as though they know everything. They show an arrogance that's off-putting to others and disrespectful to God because they believe they have all the answers for their own lives and for others' lives. Humble people know they have very few answers, and the ones they do have are because God has revealed them.

Perhaps you feel that it would be nice to have a few more answers than you do have. Knowing what's ahead might make your today easier to take. Or facing the struggles in your life would be easier if you knew the why for them. God doesn't reveal everything about life to you, but he does promise to reveal things to you that you couldn't learn any other way. Ask him the questions rolling around in your mind.

Ask him to enlighten you on the meaning of Scripture. Ask him to help you understand the why of things in your life or in the world at large. Ask. He will reveal what he knows you can handle. The rest you must take through faith in his goodness and knowledge.

18

Hope for the End of Pain

God's dwelling place is now among the people, and he will dwell with them. They will be his people, and God himself will be with them and be their God. "He will wipe every tear from their eyes. There will be no more death" or mourning or crying or pain, for the old order of things has passed away.

REVELATION 21:3–4

There's a popular vacation spot that is referred to as "The Happiest Place on Earth," and it is definitely a fun place to go. Do you wish you could live permanently in a place that is perpetually happy? A place where you have no problems and nothing can make you sad? In a place like that, there would be no reason for sadness. Does that sound too good to be true? Well, it is if you're just talking about life here on earth. But the wonderful hope you have concerns heaven. God promises to bring you to heaven someday to live with him, and any pain and struggles you've experienced here on earth will be over. He promises there will be no tears in heaven, no death and no mourning; instead there will be joy and eternal life.

What a wonderful hope that is to hang on to. When life here is painful, remember that it's only for a time and that someday there will be no more pain and sorrow. You will have only the joy of being with Jesus in heaven!

19

Conqueror in Hope

No, in all these things we are more than conquerors through him who loved us. For I am convinced that neither death nor life, neither angels nor demons, neither the present nor the future, nor any powers, neither height nor depth, nor anything else in all creation, will be able to separate us from the love of God that is in Christ Jesus our Lord.

ROMANS 8:37–39

What an amazing promise! There is nothing in the world that can pull you away from God's love. Nothing and no one is strong enough or powerful enough to make that happen. The hope of God's permanent, assured, never-changing, always-present love is so sure that you can breathe a deep sigh of relief knowing his love is yours. His love is always surrounding, protecting, guiding, and comforting you.

There may be times when you feel you've failed God or when you deliberately walk away from him. There may be times when you wonder if he wants to be done with you because you've messed up too many times. But none of those situations will make him stop loving you.

No matter how many times Satan tries to discourage you and convince you that God is done with you, he's wrong. You are the winner, the conqueror over Satan, because God promises his love for you, forever and always. So take a deep breath, get up, and get on with life. Do better today than yesterday in obeying God and loving others. You are more than a conqueror—you are God's child!

20

Hope That God Hears

Lord my God, I called to you for help,
and you healed me.

Psalm 30:2

If you have children, you know that you learn to recognize their cries. When you hear your child cry out or call for you, you learn to recognize if the situation is urgent or if they're simply frustrated or perhaps angry. You base the quickness of your response on what you determine their need to be. Sometimes, if you perceive the need isn't urgent, your child may call out over and over until you finally respond. It's a mom thing, right?

When you call out to God for help, he hears you and he answers you. You have the assured hope that God is listening. He's paying attention and not basing the urgency of his answers on how desperate you sound.

Does he always do what you want at the very moment you want his action? No, he doesn't, because he knows what you need and when it's best for you to get it in order for your faith and dependence on him to grow deeper. But just as you care for your child's needs, God cares—even more— for yours. So even as he seems to delay his response, be assured that he is with you, listening to you, loving you, and holding you close.

21

Part of the Big Picture

My dear brothers and sisters, stand firm. Let nothing move you. Always give yourselves fully to the work of the Lord, because you know that your labor in the Lord is not in vain.

1 CORINTHIANS 15:58

It's encouraging to know that what you do makes a difference. You go to work and spend your mental and physical energy to do the job, and it's nice to know it's appreciated and that in some way it contributes to the bigger picture.

This is especially true of the work you do for God's kingdom. Satan will definitely try to discourage you. He will do his best to convince you that nothing you do is important or makes a difference. It can feel like you're just spinning your wheels and never getting anywhere.

But that's not true! Look at what this verse of Scripture tells you—*nothing* you do for God is done in vain. He will use every children's story you tell, every Sunday school lesson you teach, every kind word you speak in his name, every act of service you perform for someone else, every encouraging chat you share over coffee . . . everything you do for his kingdom will be used. You may not immediately see the effect of your service—it may be one piece of a puzzle that takes years to complete—but God tells you not to lose hope, because you *are* making a difference!

22

All You Need

> *I say to myself, "The LORD is my portion;*
> *therefore I will wait for him."*
>
> LAMENTATIONS 3:24

o you sometimes think, "Well, if I had this or that thing, then I'd be fine," or "If this situation would happen or if this situation would change, then life would be better"?

Some folks live their whole lives looking for more of what they think they need instead of understanding that they have everything they really need in the Lord. In our society, accumulating more is seen as an important measure of success. Instead of being content with what they have and where they are, people keep pushing for God to do more or give them more. There is little satisfaction or contentment in their lives.

Have you come to the realization that God is all you need? Are you willing to wait for him to lead you to new places and new situations? Are you patiently waiting for him to give you what you need?

Your hope is in God, who, because of his deep love for you and his plan for your life, is truly all you need. He supplies your needs. He blesses you beyond anything you could hope for. Wait patiently for him to give you the "what's next" in your life.

23

Hope When All Seems Hopeless

While Jesus was still speaking, some people came from the house of Jairus, the synagogue leader. "Your daughter is dead," they said. "Why bother the teacher anymore?" Overhearing what they said, Jesus told him, "Don't be afraid; just believe."

MARK 5:35–36

Jairus knew his daughter was dying. That's why he went to ask Jesus for help. He knew Jesus could heal his girl, but before Jesus could do so, Jairus heard that his daughter was dead. He must have had a moment of hopelessness. Maybe he had just a moment of wondering why Jesus hadn't stopped his daughter's death. Did his faith shake just a little? If his heart had sunk, it must have bounced right back up when Jesus said, "Don't be afraid; just believe." Just like that, hope was born anew in Jairus's heart.

Maybe you've had a time when you were disappointed in God, a time when you prayed constantly for one specific situation and it felt like God didn't hear or at least didn't answer your prayer. It's hard sometimes to hold on, but faith is more than getting an immediate answer to your prayers. Faith is believing that Jesus will come through in his own good time because he knows what's best for you. So even when it is hard to wait and hard to believe, keep your hope strong in God because you know his character and his heart. Remember Jesus's words to Jairus. Faith is just believing.

24

A Life of Blessings

You make known to me the path of life;
you will fill me with joy in your presence,
with eternal pleasures at your right hand.

PSALM 16:11

Who doesn't want joy? Of course everyone does. The tension comes in trying to understand the difference between joy and happiness. Immediate pleasures bring temporary happiness, but true joy grows deep in your heart from the blessing of God's presence in your life. Joy comes from realizing that the Creator is guiding your life, that he wants to bless you and give you purpose, and that he promises eternity with him!

Hope based on God's presence and guidance in your life, as well as the blessing of being used for his work, gives great joy. God offers you the blessing of partnering with him in his work on earth—the joy of sharing his love with others and the privilege of being a part of their stories. There may be times when you make mistakes or wrong choices, but don't stress over them or over what the future holds. Learn from the past and keep moving forward. You can trust God, who holds your life in his hands. This true joy allows you the freedom to notice the many blessings God gives you—even the ordinary, everyday things that are gifts from him.

25

Life's Guidebook

All Scripture is God-breathed and is useful for teaching, rebuking, correcting and training in righteousness, so that the servant of God may be thoroughly equipped for every good work.

2 TIMOTHY 3:16–17

You do not need to have all the answers. Is that a relief or what? In fact, it's virtually impossible for you to have the answers for all the situations you face in life. What you need is wisdom that comes from a greater source than your own mind. This comes as no surprise to God; that's why you have the Bible at your disposal. God's wisdom for anything you need to know is contained in Scripture.

Scripture answers any questions you may have about obeying God and what it means to be submitted to him so that your life is focused only on serving him. Scripture teaches you how to live in community with others, loving and serving them as God would have you do. God guides you through specific situations in life by making his Word come alive to you at just the right moment to answer a question you are struggling with. When you read God's Word with a submitted heart, he shows you when you are doing things that do not honor him.

God's Word prepares you for a life of service to him by helping you come to know him better. Everything you need to know is in his Word.

26

Hope in a New Attitude

We are God's handiwork, created in Christ Jesus to do good works, which God prepared in advance for us to do.

EPHESIANS 2:10

What's your crabby quotient? Do you start off each day with a chip on your shoulder? What causes it? Feeling unappreciated? Too much work? Not enjoying your work? Feeling like you just don't matter . . . even to God? Whoa. Stop right there. You matter to God in bigger ways than you can imagine.

What does the word *handiwork* conjure up in your mind? Perhaps you think of creative work done by hand, such as knitting or crocheting. Maybe it's the talents of someone who paints lovely pictures, sews, or builds things. Almost certainly handiwork is something made by hand, which means the creator of that piece has put time and energy into making it. Each piece of handiwork is special to its creator because it is work from the heart, and the creator has a personal in-vestment in it.

Here's where the "you matter to God" comes into play. You are his handiwork. He made you with a special job in mind through which you can serve him, and he's already equipped you to do that job. You are special to him because he made you. He equipped you. He has something special for you to do. So keep your crabby attitude at bay, and serve God in joy.

27

Growing Older and Wiser

Teach us to number our days,
that we may gain a heart of wisdom.
PSALM 90:12

How do you feel about growing older? Are you dropping bundles of money on creams that promise to slow down the look of aging? Or hair coloring to push away the gray? Do you fight the middle-age bulge to keep your youthful figure? It's a lot of work and expense to try to appear youthful when you're not.

Of course it's a good thing to take care of yourself so you stay as healthy as possible into your mature years. But instead of focusing only on staying young, perhaps it's better to embrace aging and appreciate the wisdom you've gained from living as long as you have. Take hope in that wisdom so you can share it with the young people in your life and save them from having to learn some things the hard way. The wisdom you've gained in life teaches you to become a better person, to focus on what really matters, to not sweat the small stuff, to make God your priority, and to treat people with kindness and respect. The wisdom gained through the experience of living life makes your golden years all the more golden. Start as young as you can to gain wisdom with each year of living.

28

Hope in a Strong Finish

Being confident of this, that he who began a good work in you will carry it on to completion until the day of Christ Jesus.

PHILIPPIANS 1:6

The older you get, the faster the years fly by, right? In the blink of an eye your toddler is in high school or you're a decade older or a "young" friend is retiring. Like most folks, you probably have things on your radar that you plan to do someday. Not just vacations or home improvements but things that are service or ministry focused, things you feel will really matter in the big scheme of life and to God's kingdom. Then one day you glance at the calendar and realize that time has been flying by and you have not done any of those things. That's discouraging, isn't it?

Well, here's a solid hope for you—God isn't finished with you yet! He knows how quickly the years are passing. He's paying attention and, without a doubt, he is using you to bless others in ways you may not even recognize. The wonderful thing about serving God is that sometimes you are intentional in what you do, and he has specific work for you, but even when you aren't intentional, he still uses your talents and gifts to bless others and to share his love. One thing you'll never retire from is serving God!

29

Hope for the Growth of the Kingdom

This is what the kingdom of God is like. A man scatters seed on the ground. Night and day, whether he sleeps or gets up, the seed sprouts and grows, though he does not know how.

MARK 4:26–27

It sometimes feels like the evil one is winning. When you hear the news of wars and hatred around the world, it's frightening. Even more discouraging are the reports of evil done one-on-one when people are assaulted or murdered. Why isn't the message of God's love stopping people from such wickedness?

You also hear of Christians being persecuted around the world and forced into secrecy. Why doesn't God prevent that?

The hope you must grab on to is that God's kingdom is actually growing. It may be slow. It may be under the radar.

But nothing done for God is wasted. Hearts are changed and challenged. Even in places around the world where the church is forced underground, believers' faith is growing stronger. God will not be defeated!

Don't be discouraged. Keep hope! Stay strong in your faith, living for Christ. Stay strong in praying for Christians around the world and in giving to ministries that are making a difference. Stay strong in praying against the evil that people do to one another. Stay strong in your own service to God. God's kingdom will survive and prosper!

30

Hope of Purpose

*Therefore we do not lose heart. Though outwardly we are
wasting away, yet inwardly we are being renewed day by day.
For our light and momentary troubles are achieving for us an
eternal glory that far outweighs them all. So we fix our eyes
not on what is seen, but on what is unseen, since what is seen is
temporary, but what is unseen is eternal.*

2 Corinthians 4:16–18

Perhaps you aren't at the stage of life where you feel that
you're physically or mentally wasting away. If you do
feel somewhat that way, then hopefully you'll have a reener-
gizing phase. As time passes and you see yourself changing,
it's tempting to think that you no longer have much purpose.
But regardless of what's happening to your body, God still
has a plan for the rest of your life.

Don't just focus on what your body can't do anymore.
Whatever is going on with it is only a part of who you are.

Sure, there are things you can't do right now, but God says there are more important things happening. Your eternal glory is still being developed. Work on your attitude by asking God to show you what your purpose is for him this day. Don't let physical limitations discourage you. Keep your heart focused on Jesus because what he's teaching you is what's most important. He still has a purpose for your life. It may be different than it was before, but it's just as important!

31

Hope through No Prejudice

> Do not forget to show hospitality to strangers, for by so doing some people have shown hospitality to angels without knowing it.
>
> HEBREWS 13:2

Be kind. Just be kind. It shouldn't be that hard, but for some people it seems to be. They find it difficult to be kind and gracious to anyone who is even a little different from them. That's too bad because they may be missing a huge blessing by being so standoffish.

If you knew that the homeless person asking for a handout was an angel, wouldn't you hand them a twenty-dollar bill? If someone from another country and another religion needed a question answered about living in this country, and if you knew that person was an angel, you'd kindly speak to them and give answers, right?

You see, that's the thing. Your prejudices against certain groups of people may be hurting you more than they hurt them. Show the love of Christ to *all* you come in contact with. You may bless an angel, and you will definitely show love that is reflective of God's love. If you happen to help another person, well that's good too, because you will be blessed in the process!

32

Firewall of Hope

You, LORD, are a shield around me,
my glory, the One who lifts my head high.
PSALM 3:3

Websites are protected by firewalls. A firewall is sort of like a shield. It determines who can and can't get through to the website based on predetermined security rules. Protection is important.

It's nice to know you have protection when you need it—and you do have it! If you've asked Jesus to be your Savior, his Holy Spirit has come into your heart, and he is with you constantly. He never leaves you. The Holy Spirit protects your heart, which is the core of your being. The condition of your heart affects your thoughts and actions. So the Bible tells you to guard your heart because it's so important to your mental and spiritual well-being. The Holy Spirit is a holy firewall around your heart.

More than that, God is the shield around you. He watches out for you. He protects you more times each day than you can probably even imagine. Nothing happens to you without God's knowledge. He is your shield against the world and against Satan's efforts to harm you or pull you away from God. Depend on God. Talk to him. Tell him what you need and go forward with courage knowing that he is protecting you!

33

Hope in Being Heard

This is the confidence we have in approaching God: that if we ask anything according to his will, he hears us. And if we know that he hears us—whatever we ask—we know that we have what we asked of him.

1 John 5:14–15

It means a lot when you feel that you are being heard. When you have a conversation with some people, they appear to be preoccupied, busy with their phone, or just not paying attention to you. So when you engage in conversation with someone who gives you their full attention and cares about what you say, you feel heard and valued as a person.

It's something to have another person value you enough to listen to you, but it's even more amazing when you realize that God himself listens when you speak to him. He gives you his complete attention. He wants to hear what you have to say to him.

Even more wonderful is that if you stay close to God so that your heart is submitted to him, then you trust his plans for you, so as you pray, you're asking him to do what he really wants to do. Be assured that he will not only hear your prayers but answer them and guide every step you take.

Thank God for listening to your prayers. Thank him for caring enough to hear you.

34

Hope in Closeness

Come near to God and he will come near to you.

JAMES 4:8

There's comfort in being close to someone you love. Hopefully as a child you had the opportunity to snuggle close to someone as they read a book to you. Or perhaps you've been the adult reader with a child or grandchild squeezed in close. There's comfort in a hug from someone you love when you need encouragement. There's also comfort in just sitting with someone—no words needed—just being near someone who you know cares about you.

When you need comfort or encouragement, draw near to God. Go to a quiet place alone and meditate on his love for you. Give yourself time to put aside all the things clamoring for your attention and care. Push those things aside and think about God and his love for you. Choose a Bible verse about his care for you that's especially meaningful to you, and really think about it. When you come near to him, he meets you there. He promised he would. There is no greater hope for comfort than to know that you are in God's presence and that he loves you completely and unconditionally. Be still with him. Let his love flow over you.

35

Hope in Secret Giving

When you give to the needy, do not let your left hand know what your right hand is doing, so that your giving may be in secret. Then your Father, who sees what is done in secret, will reward you.

MATTHEW 6:3–4

Secret blessings are such a joy! If you've ever been the recipient of an anonymous gift, you know how wonderful it feels to know that someone cares enough to give you a gift. It means that the giver is paying attention to you—to what you need or to what you like. It also means that the giver is not giving the gift in order to be thanked or to receive praise for their generosity. The giver just wants to bless you.

Are you a secret gift-giver? Giving in secret without hoping for recognition or praise is truly sacrificial giving. When you give completely from the goodness of your heart, God will reward that generosity. His reward will probably not be a monetary reward, but whatever it is, it will include the joyous blessing of knowing you have helped another person in some way.

So don't give to the needy just for the tax break. Don't give so that you get a pat on the back. Don't give expecting anything in return. Give from a heart that is grateful for the blessings you have, and hope for a "well done" from the Lord when you meet him in heaven.

36

Hope in God's GPS

*I have hidden your word in my heart
that I might not sin against you.*

PSALM 119:11

You need to get from Point A to Point B. There are several possible routes, but how do you know which one is best? You could drive around trying various routes, getting lost, taking hours of time, using lots of gas, and possibly giving up in frustration and never reaching your destination. Or you could grab a map and outline the streets to take from Point A to Point B. Maybe you could plug the addresses into your GPS and let its gentle voice tell you, "Drive straight. Turn left. You have arrived at your destination."

If only life were that simple. If only there were a map or GPS to guide your choices, behaviors, attitudes, and actions. There is! It's called the Bible. It is your map, your GPS for guiding you in how to be successful in living for God. Reading the stories in it helps you to learn God's character and shows you how he interacts with his people. His Word gives you guidelines for honoring, obeying, and worshiping him and for living in community with others. It challenges you to love others and honor them with your service.

God's desire is that you will memorize verses from his Word so that its wisdom is readily available to you for whatever challenges life brings. God's Word is your guide and your comfort all at the same time!

37

Blessed Hope

The grace of God has appeared that offers salvation to all people. It teaches us to say "No" to ungodliness and worldly passions, and to live self-controlled, upright and godly lives in this present age, while we wait for the blessed hope—the appearing of the glory of our great God and Savior, Jesus Christ.

TITUS 2:11–13

The blessed hope of Jesus's return to take you to heaven—what a glorious thing to anticipate! Do you spend your days standing, looking heavenward while believing that Jesus might come back at any moment? Probably not, because of, well . . . life. But you should live with that anticipation always in your mind so that it flavors all you do and every choice you make.

How you live in the here and now reflects what you truly believe about the blessed hope of Jesus's return. That's a sobering thought, isn't it? It's true though, because if you believe that Jesus could return at any moment, then you will be careful how you live. You will choose to turn away from actions and choices that do not honor God. The things the world offers you as fun or rewarding but that do not align with living for God will not be so tempting. You will choose to honor God and to love others as he instructed. You will be self-controlled about serving and obeying him because the most important thing is to be guiltless when Jesus returns. That truly will make his return a blessed hope!

38

Reflecting Jesus's Love

May the God who gives endurance and encouragement give you the same attitude of mind toward each other that Christ Jesus had, so that with one mind and one voice you may glorify the God and Father of our Lord Jesus Christ.

ROMANS 15:5–6

Do you play nice with others? If not, why not? Okay, some people are more of a challenge to love than others. Some people choose to be critical and judgmental, which makes them no fun to be around. Their negative attitudes may seep into your own behavior, too, and you certainly don't want that.

If there are people you have difficulty treating in the same way Jesus did, ask God for help. How did Jesus treat others? He was kind to those who were struggling, helping them as only he could. He gave to them. He spent time with them.

Of course, he also held accountable those who needed to be held accountable.

For those you have trouble being kind to, ask Jesus for his help and strength to be kind. Ask him to help you see the good in those people and to be able to concentrate on that.

Make it your goal to reflect Jesus to all with whom you come in contact. Yes, at times you'll need his help to be patient and kind. But you will be glorifying God and sharing his love through your behavior.

39

Hope of a Clean Slate

Repent, then, and turn to God, so that your sins may be wiped out, that times of refreshing may come from the Lord.

ACTS 3:19

Whew. Have there been times when you just wanted to start over? Maybe a day has gotten off to a bad start, and you just want to start anew. Or maybe you've really messed up in a friendship and you want a do-over. Of course, in all that starting over, you want your mistakes and wrongs to be totally forgotten. Otherwise it wouldn't be a clean slate. However, wiping the slate clean is a hard thing for people to do. They may be okay with forgiving the ways you've hurt them, but forgetting? Well, that's a different story.

The human reticence to forget being wronged makes God's ability to forgive *and* forget even more of a blessing. You have the hope of a clean slate with God, time after time after time! When you repent—turn away from your sin—he forgives and forgets. He wipes out the sin and the *memory* of the sin. What a blessing! This is God's love in action. When you repent of your sin, he wants to believe the best of you, and he gives you the opportunity to move forward with a clean slate.

40

Don't Be Afraid

> *Have I not commanded you? Be strong and courageous. Do not be afraid; do not be discouraged, for the LORD your God will be with you wherever you go.*
>
> JOSHUA 1:9

What scares you? What makes you weak in the knees and afraid to face a new day? Maybe you're afraid of failure in a difficult job or even in a relationship. Maybe you're afraid of a partner or of someone who is bullying you or stalking you. Maybe you're afraid of disappointing God.

You're told over and over in Scripture not to be afraid . . . *fear not . . . be courageous . . . be strong.* So, why is it so hard? God promises over and over to be with you and that he will never leave you. He is protecting you, guiding you, strengthening you. Why is life still frightening?

The bottom line is that, for whatever reason, it just is sometimes. But each time you need to be strong, read the verses that promise you God's presence and strength. Be reminded that you are never, ever alone. There is no actual reason to be afraid or discouraged, because God, who is more powerful than anything or anyone, is with you, fighting for you, guarding you, loving you. Stay focused on him!

41

A Humble Heart

When you pray, go into your room, close the door and pray to your Father, who is unseen. Then your Father, who sees what is done in secret, will reward you.

MATTHEW 6:6

God values a humble follower and judges a person who functions on pride. Some Christians make a big show of their Christianity, but their hearts aren't submitted to God. They live with pride in themselves and are judgmental and critical of others. Often they're more concerned with what others think of them than with what God thinks.

To have hope in pleasing God, submit your heart to him and be humble. Don't make a show of your relationship with him; in fact, God says to do your serious personal prayer time in private. Of course praying with others is a good thing too. But when you're pouring out the secrets in your heart, keep it between you and God. The intense personal conversations you have with him will grow your faith and trust in him. The goal of your prayer life is to share the depths of your soul with him. That's something that should be done in private, not as a show before others. God will hear the desires of your humble heart, and he will reward your trust in him.

42

A Servant's Heart

The LORD is my shepherd, I lack nothing.
PSALM 23:1

There's a song in the well-loved musical *Fiddler on the Roof* about Tevye's dream of being a wealthy man. One line in that song asks this question: "Would it spoil some vast eternal plan if I were a wealthy man?"* Maybe you ask that, too, as the financial stresses of life weigh down on you. How does God decide who should be blessed with material comforts while others have to struggle to make ends meet?

Perhaps God isn't concerned with how much money you have. His focus is on giving you what you need so that you can become more like Jesus. What does that mean? It means he gives you a servant's heart and a selfless compassion for others. As a Christ follower, you humbly submit to God's will

* Jerry Bock and Sheldon Harnick, "If I Were a Rich Man," *Fiddler on the Roof*, © 1964.

for your life because you trust him completely, and you love others—even those who are different from you—as much as you love yourself.

The wonderful thing is that God guides and leads you through this growth journey because of his love for you. You have the hope of becoming more like Jesus because God gives you everything you need for the process.

43

No Half-Hearted Searching

You will seek me and find me when you seek me with all your heart.

JEREMIAH 29:13

A half-hearted commitment to Jesus simply will not work. Scripture tells you that God won't share your heart with any other thing or person; he must be Number One in your heart. Loving and serving God will only enhance your life and make all other things in your life even more wonderful.

Do you hope to know God more deeply and honestly? That happens by submitting to him and asking him to push all other things aside so that he is most important to you. That is a moment-by-moment process as personal priorities keep pushing their way back into your focus. Your submission will be repeated over and over as Satan continuously pushes other things ahead of God, trying to pull you away from serving him.

The wonderful hope you have is that as you submit to God and allow him to rule in your heart, you will be blessed to know him more and more deeply. He loves you very much, and fully loving him will be an amazing blessing to you.

44

Hope in Another's Prayers

Confess your sins to each other and pray for each other so that you may be healed. The prayer of a righteous person is powerful and effective.

JAMES 5:16

Are you supposed to confess your sins to anyone who will listen? Should it be a public broadcast? Of course not. God wants you to live in community with other believers. You need to hold one another accountable in your Christian walk and to encourage one another in your faith. A group of friends with whom you have an intimate spiritual relationship is the place where you can share your failings as well as your victories and the lessons you're learning.

One of the blessings of living in community with other believers is the privilege of praying for one another. When you confess your sins, your friends commit to praying for you and helping you to overcome those sins, and you can do the same for them. In that way you become a part of one another's Christian walk so your bonds of unity go even deeper.

God promises to hear the prayers of his children. He also says that the prayers of those who are seeking to know him in a deep and meaningful way and who love one another with a humble, sincere love will get results. Your prayers are powerfully strong in getting things done!

45

Hope in the Stillness

Be still, and know that I am God;
I will be exalted among the nations,
I will be exalted in the earth.

PSALM 46:10

As a believer, do you hope for God's kingdom to grow so that more and more people will know him? Of course you do. Do you know your role in making that happen? You have one. God gives every believer a job to do. One way of helping the message of God's love spread around the world is something so simple that perhaps you've never thought about its importance . . . be still.

In the chaos of the world you live in, there are constantly voices shouting information at you or demanding your attention and your allegiance. It's hard to think with all the noise, and it's hard to know which voices to listen to and which ones speak truth. God says to be quiet and wait for his voice to stand out. Then you'll know which voice to follow. As your heart turns to God in the quietness, you will be amazed at his greatness, power, and love. That amazement will be hard to keep to yourself, so you will likely want to share your love for God with others. That's how your stillness plays a role in telling the world about God.

46

Hope in Weakness

My grace is sufficient for you, for my power is made perfect in weakness.

2 CORINTHIANS 12:9

This verse seems like an oxymoron, doesn't it? The idea that your weakness makes God's power perfect seems strange. But when you realize that your weakness provides the opportunity for God's power to shine, then it makes sense.

When you try to power through life in your own strength, God doesn't get credit for the things that are happening. You may say that you need him and trust him, but your devotion is not evident by your actions. When others see your pride in your own abilities, they know that God is not the source of your power.

But when you admit your weaknesses and your need for God to take over your heart, then by his grace . . . he does. His power becomes your power. His strength becomes your strength. By your words, actions, and heart devotion, God receives the credit for your strength in overcoming weakness. He gets the praise for healing your heart wounds. His strength is what enables you to do his work. God loving others through you is apparent to all around you, and his power is perfected by your weakness because you acknowledge your need for him.

47

Over-the-Top Power

Now to him who is able to do immeasurably more than all we ask or imagine, according to his power that is at work within us, to him be glory in the church and in Christ Jesus throughout all generations, for ever and ever! Amen.

EPHESIANS 3:20–21

When you were a child, did you make a wish list for birthday or Christmas gifts? Those lists are usually filled with anything you can think of—over-the-top big gifts (after all, it is a *wish* list) and practical, more affordable gifts. You probably didn't have much hope of receiving the over-the-top big gift, but it never hurt to try. After all, Grandma might come through.

There is one time when you will receive more than you ask for, more than you ever expect to get. God is the over-the-top gift giver. His unlimited power works in your heart to make you more like Jesus—loving, humble, and obedient to God. His power in your life makes things possible that you never even dared to dream, and it gives you unimaginable courage and strength.

Whatever God does in your life is to glorify himself for all to see. When you submit to his power, you have the blessing of playing a part in his kingdom being grown throughout the world!

48

Hope in Grace-Filled Speech

Let your conversation be always full of grace, seasoned with salt, so that you may know how to answer everyone.

COLOSSIANS 4:6

The Bible often mentions the power of words. What you say to others and how you speak—the tone and attitude of your words—matter. This verse tells you to make sure your words are full of grace. What does it mean to speak words of grace? It hearkens back to "Do unto others as you would have them do unto you," doesn't it? Speak words of kindness, lifting others up and reinforcing all that is good in them. Compliment jobs well done and efforts made. Encourage others to try new things, challenging them to keep on going when things get tough.

Your grace-filled conversation should be comforting, filled with compassion for what those around you are going through. Your love, which reflects God's love, begins with what and how you speak to others; from there, let your actions reinforce your words.

Salt-seasoned words of grace are encouraging, challenging, loving words that share the truth of God's love and draw others to him. They reflect your relationship with Jesus and how you value other people. Be careful about the words you speak. Your words have power, so use your power for good by speaking kindly.

49

Life Dreams

> "My thoughts are not your thoughts,
>   neither are your ways my ways," declares
>   the LORD.
> "As the heavens are higher than the earth,
>   so are my ways higher than your ways
>   and my thoughts than your thoughts."
>
> ISAIAH 55:8–9

It's good to have a dream for your future life—a dream career, a dream marriage, dream children, a dream retirement. Of course everyone dreams of the best life, and there is nothing wrong with that. But your well-laid plans will probably not go as you hope. Plans seldom do.

What's your response when you realize that what you expected your life to be is never going to happen? Instead of getting upset, think about it this way: God has a much better plan for your life than you do. After all, God knows the expanse of your whole life—people you will meet, choices you will make, careers you will have, family you will have. He knows how all those things will play into making you the person you become. He knows the plans he has for you and the ways you will be a part of others' lives.

Embrace his plan for your life and celebrate with hope that his plan is better, more exciting, and more fulfilling than even your best dream ever could have been!

50

Hope in Silence

Even fools are thought wise if they keep silent,
and discerning if they hold their tongues.

PROVERBS 17:28

Do you hope that other people think you're wise? Would you like to be a person other people come to for advice? There's a simple way to appear wise, even as you're gaining the wisdom that comes with age, and that is to keep quiet. Easier said than done for some folks, right? But the fact is that sometimes when you spout out opinions or advice without being asked or without having the full story, you appear foolish.

But keeping quiet and listening to what others say makes you appear wise. It also shows that you are interested in other people and their opinions. You are willing to listen to them and hear their stories. You care what situations they are dealing with.

While you are keeping quiet, spend time in Scripture and seek God's wisdom for life. Be careful to listen to his Spirit instructing and guiding you as to when to speak and how to present your comments. Share God's wisdom . . . not yours.

51

Hope for Contentment

Keep your lives free from the love of money and be content with what you have, because God has said,

> *"Never will I leave you;*
> *never will I forsake you."*

HEBREWS 13:5

No matter how much money a person has, it never seems to be enough. The goal is to get more. The love of money becomes an addiction so that time and effort is focused on having more of it. It puts your priority on work over time with family, friends, and even God.

Why is money so important? Why is there never enough? Why is it so hard to be content? Our culture screams that you need more, more, more, which makes it very hard to be content with just having enough for what you need. Those always striving for more are seldom content.

Contentment is being happy with what God gives you. It means you are satisfied with having enough to meet your needs and with sharing any excess with those who don't have enough. Sometimes you even make do with less and share from funds you actually need in order to help someone else. Being content allows you to give others hope through your generosity.

52

Hope from Living Water

Jesus answered, "Everyone who drinks this water will be thirsty again, but whoever drinks the water I give them will never thirst. Indeed, the water I give them will become in them a spring of water welling up to eternal life."

JOHN 4:13–14

Jesus warned against drinking the water of deception. What was he talking about? He was warning against putting your faith in anything or anyone other than him. Some people get sucked into believing whatever the popular thoughts are, whether they honor God or not. Those popular ideas come and go, so it's hard to build a life on them.

The hope for true joy and contentment is found only in believing that Jesus is God's Son who came to earth to live as a human being and to die for your sins. He rose again, and his Holy Spirit lives in your heart to teach and guide you to obey God and live for him. That belief is the water you can drink that will give you the hope of eternal life and contentment deep in your heart. That contentment grows and deepens as your understanding of him grows. Since he never changes, you can count on him for the rest of your life. Just as Jesus said, giving your heart to him and believing in Scripture becomes a bubbling well of life in your heart.

53

Hope in God's Power

> The LORD is the great God,
>   the great King above all gods.
> In his hand are the depths of the earth,
>   and the mountain peaks belong to him.
> The sea is his, for he made it,
>   and his hands formed the dry land.
>
> PSALM 95:3–5

Are you fascinated by creation? What part of God's creation speaks most clearly to you of his creative power? Is it the majestic rugged mountains that seem to reach to the heavens or the massive oceans with crashing waves? Maybe it's the flat prairies with waves of grasses and grains gently blowing, or giant sequoia trees or meandering brooks. Do you look at impressive thunderstorms with flashing lightning or at stars shooting across the night sky and immediately marvel at God's creativity and awesome power?

The very first verse in the Bible gives God the credit for everything in our world, even in the universe. It was all made by his hand and came from his great mind. All creation speaks of his mighty power, from storms, volcanoes, and earthquakes to tiny hummingbirds and gentle butterflies. His power controls all of these. Just a word from him and the sun stands still, a storm stops, a river divides, or a bush burns.

That amazing power is where you put your hope because it is the power of *your* Creator . . . God, who loves you!

54

Hope of Loving a Difficult Person

We love because he first loved us.
1 JOHN 4:19

*A*rrgghh! Have you ever wanted to just walk away from a person and cut her out of your life? A friend— or family member—who knows just how to push your buttons and totally frustrate you can make life unpleasant. Maybe she knows how annoying she is, and she does it on purpose just to get a reaction from you. Ugh. No fun. So you take the high road and just push her out of your daily life, avoiding her as much as possible. How are you supposed to love someone who is basically unlovable?

There is only one hope for being able to love someone like that: God. It *is* possible to love a difficult person by allowing God's love to flow through you. Think about it . . . you aren't always lovable, but God constantly loves you. Sometimes you deliberately disobey God, but he doesn't stop loving you. His example of love is constant, steady, forgiving, and selfless. You can have the hope of loving a difficult person by asking God to love through you over and over until one day you realize that you do, in fact, actually love that person!

55

Hope of Family

See what great love the Father has lavished on us, that we should be called children of God! And that is what we are!

1 JOHN 3:1

Our families can be wonderful or flawed and usually are a mix of both. Our times together can include laughter or tears, good advice or bad examples, but one thing is for sure—we know who's family and who's not. We know where we belong and who our tribe is.

When you accept Christ as your Savior, you are adopted into God's family. You are a child of the King, and being a member of his family is amazing! Your heavenly Father loves you even more than your earthly family does, and he is happy to call you his child. As you learn more and more about him you will see the evidence of his DNA in your heart. The familial characteristics will be obvious in the way you love others in humility and self-denial.

Whatever your earthly family is like, you belong to the family of God.

Celebrate your position in his family by learning about your Father and how you can reflect his DNA to those around you.

56

Clothed in Love

Therefore, as God's chosen people, holy and dearly loved, clothe yourselves with compassion, kindness, humility, gentleness and patience. Bear with each other and forgive one another if any of you has a grievance against someone. Forgive as the Lord forgave you. And over all these virtues put on love, which binds them all together in perfect unity.

COLOSSIANS 3:12–14

It shouldn't be hard to be nice, should it? You are a child of God. His DNA is flowing through your veins and one of his major characteristics is love. How can you love others the way that God does? How can you even hope to love that well? God lists the characteristics of his love in these verses. None of them are really difficult. To clothe yourself with these characteristics means you have to intentionally put them on just as you put on the pieces of your physical clothing each day.

Treat those around you with compassion, which means showing you care about the struggles they face. Be kind in the way you treat others, especially the way you speak to them. Be humble and lift others up. Be gentle in all you say and do. Be patient with those who don't do things the way you would do them. Bear with them in their mistakes and the learning process as they are maturing. Forgive when you must and, more than anything else, love others. Just love. When you do these things, you have the hope of being united with others by your love for Christ.

57

All In

> *Trust in the LORD with all your heart*
> *and lean not on your own understanding;*
> *in all your ways submit to him,*
> *and he will make your paths straight.*
>
> PROVERBS 3:5–6

When you are part of a team or club, it is expected that your loyalty and support will be to that group. It's not really a good idea to try to split your support between your team and a competitor. You can't fully support both of them. You're either all in or you're not in at all.

Your relationship with God is an all-in or not-in-at-all kind of thing too. God doesn't want you to sort of trust him; he wants all your trust—about everything—from deep in your whole heart because you know that God is the only and best way. No one else you trust has your best interest in mind. You can't even trust yourself more than you trust him. He has a better understanding of the world, your life, and his work than you do. So trust him enough to submit to him. That means you let him have control of your life, and you don't resist his guidance or plan. You have to fully trust him in order to do that. When you're all in for God, your heart belongs to him and your trust is in him. He will guide and direct your life.

58

Hope for Rescue

> *Be strong, do not fear;*
> *your God will come,*
> *   he will come with vengeance;*
> *with divine retribution*
> *   he will come to save you.*
>
> ISAIAH 35:4

Numerous times Scripture tells you to "fear not." Just don't be afraid. But the reality is that you will run into some pretty stress-inducing situations in life, and some of them can be overwhelming. When your heart is afraid, your trust in God is tested. That's when you know how deep your trust is and whether you really believe he has your back. Times of testing offer times of growth. If God rescues you when there is nothing frightening happening, it doesn't seem like such a big deal. But when you're scared or things look hopeless and you see God show up to save you—even push your enemies away from you—then you know that he's taking care of you. You know you can trust him.

The more often you see God rescue you, the easier it will be to trust him more deeply. Step out in faith and trust him with whatever you are facing today. See his protection, and then the next time you're afraid, trust will come a bit easier. Trust is a growth process, and the reward is no fear!

59

Hope in God's Nearness

The LORD is near to all who call on him,
to all who call on him in truth.

PSALM 145:18

A large crowded room, like an auditorium or a stadium, is a cacophony of noise. Voices shouting to be heard above the roar make it hard to have a conversation at all. If you should happen to get separated from the ones you came with, it may take awhile to find them again. You might notice your friend through the crowd of people and call out to her, even shout to get her attention so you can reunite with her. But with all the people and noise, she can't hear you and doesn't even see you. Getting back together is going to be a challenge.

That will never happen with God. He promises that when you call out to him, he will come right to you, as close as possible. His closeness means he is protecting, guiding, and loving you.

It is a wonderful hope that God is always available to you. He loves you so much, and he wants to be close to you. He's actually happy when you call to him, so call to him daily and believe that he will come.

60

Stay Alert!

Be alert and of sober mind. Your enemy the devil prowls around like a roaring lion looking for someone to devour. Resist him, standing firm in the faith, because you know that the family of believers throughout the world is undergoing the same kind of sufferings.

1 PETER 5:8–9

Pay attention! Don't let your guard down. Don't ever let yourself get too comfortable, feeling like you've got a handle on this faith stuff. That lack of focus is just what Satan is watching for. He's always looking for a chink in your armor where he can sneak in and do his work of pulling you away from God. His hunger to do that is never satisfied. He wants to pull more and more believers away from their faith in God.

Don't let Satan win! Stand firm by staying connected to Jesus. Read his Word. Don't just read it; meditate on it, learn it, and let it sink deep into your heart so that you can gain strength by pulling its words up in your memory when you feel tempted or hopeless. Quoting Scripture is one major way you defeat the devil. He has no response to it.

Take comfort in the fact that you aren't the only person Satan is after. Every believer in the whole world has to fight a battle against him. Stay alert and serious about your relationship with God.

61

Lavished with Blessings

In him we have redemption through his blood, the forgiveness of sins, in accordance with the riches of God's grace that he lavished on us.

EPHESIANS 1:7–8

ou are redeemed because Jesus died on the cross. What does *redeemed* mean? It means your sins have been compensated for . . . the price has been paid by Jesus's shed blood on the cross. Because you are redeemed, your sins are forgiven. There are no penalties you need to pay. It's pretty awesome that your sins won't come back to haunt you somewhere down the road. By God's grace they are gone . . . forever forgotten. God has taken care of everything for you. He has made you a member of his family and blesses you abundantly every day.

There's a beautiful word in these verses . . . *lavished*. You see, God didn't just give you the basics of what you need or offer the very minimum of blessings. No, he turned the blessings jar upside down and poured them out. He blessed you with his grace more than you could have dreamed, more than you ever expected, more than you could imagine. He loves you so much that he just wants to give you more and more blessings, grace, and love.

62

True Love

I love those who love me,
and those who seek me find me.
PROVERBS 8:17

It's a beautiful thing to be in love. When you are newly in love, you want to be with the one who is the object of your affection all the time. You long to hear what your love is thinking, what he likes to do, where he likes to go, what food he likes to eat. You want to know everything about him. You never get enough! It's wonderful.

Do you love God like that? Do you long to spend time with him? Do you want to know everything about him? Do you read his Word to learn his character and his likes and dislikes? It's all there for you. Just as spending time with your loved one is the best way to get to know him, the only way to get to know God is to spend time with him. The beauty of reaching out to get to know God is that he eagerly meets you, and he loves you even more than you love him! The hope of loving God is the certainty that he loves you. There is no unrequited love with him! He promises that when you look for him, you will find him. God wants to be with you!

63

Hoping for What You Don't Have Yet

We ourselves, who have the firstfruits of the Spirit, groan inwardly as we wait eagerly for our adoption to sonship, the redemption of our bodies. For in this hope we were saved. But hope that is seen is no hope at all. Who hopes for what they already have?

ROMANS 8:23–24

Being a Christian and learning to know God better means that you long to do better in your efforts to live for him. You long to obey him more consistently. You long to love the way he loves—to love him and to love others. Your mind knows that on this earth you will never achieve the perfection you hope for. But you have the hope of Jesus coming back to take you to heaven. When you get to heaven, you will no longer sin. You will no longer struggle with staying close to God or with moving forward in the process of becoming more like Jesus. You will have everything you have hoped for.

You have to wait for the reward of heaven, and you have no clue as to when it will come. So you wait. Waiting isn't easy, is it? You hope for heaven, but you don't have it yet; if you did, there would be no need to hope for it. In the meantime, your responsibility is to get to know God as well as you can and to grow in the process of learning to obey him. It's a wonderful hope, and it's worth waiting for.

64

Hope for Victory over Death

When the perishable has been clothed with the imperishable, and the mortal with immortality, then the saying that is written will come true: "Death has been swallowed up in victory."

"Where, O death, is your victory?
Where, O death, is your sting?"

1 CORINTHIANS 15:54–55

eath is a difficult part of life, but it's a necessary part. No one lives forever, as painful as that is. It hurts when you must say goodbye to a loved one who dies. It hurts for a long time. Death happens because humans sinned. It wasn't a part of God's original plan for us.

But because Jesus died to pay the price for humankind's sins, there is hope. When God raised Jesus back to life, he showed his power over death and proved that death doesn't win. It isn't the end. One day all God's followers will be alive in heaven—those who died here on earth and those who are caught up to heaven before they die. Death is defeated!

What a wonderful hope you have. It's okay to be sad when a loved one dies—you're sad because you loved. But don't be without hope. Death is not the end!

65

The Feast Is Coming!

You prepare a table before me
*   in the presence of my enemies.*
You anoint my head with oil;
*   my cup overflows.*

PSALM 23:5

ew people get through life without making someone
angry once in a while. You may experience criticism or
antagonism from others simply because you follow Jesus.
Satan will feed their criticism because he will do whatever he
can to give you trouble. He wants you to turn away from God.

But the hope of victory is yours because God has your
back! He will not allow you to be permanently defeated by
your—or his—enemies. What could be more victorious
than God preparing a feast for you as a big celebration of
the fact that you are part of his family? Your enemies can
only stand and watch the party. They can't stop it. They can't
join in. They can only watch! How cool is that? While you

are feasting at God's table, they stand nearby, hungry and frustrated.

God always wins, and because he is protecting and guarding you, you always win too. There may be times when it doesn't feel like you're winning. Victory may seem far off, but be patient and trust God. Keep your fork in hand because the party is coming!

66

Getting through Stress

Cast all your anxiety on him because he cares for you.
1 PETER 5:7

Worry, fear, and anxiety all affect you in some way. These effects show in different ways with everyone. When some people get worried, they sleep all the time. Others can't sleep at all. Some eat junk food nonstop. Others can't eat anything. Some function normally and keep everything inside. Others cannot function at all and cry constantly.

Is there a better way to handle anxiety and worry? Yes, give it to God. Just tell him what's worrying you, and ask him to take care of it. Will he fix the problem? Maybe not, but he will give you the necessary strength to face it. God can help you get through stress without losing sleep or gaining (or losing) weight. His presence gives you the assurance that everything is going to be okay. You may have to intentionally give the problem to God daily or hourly—not because he doesn't help you, but because you keep grabbing it back to worry about. Each time it pops into your mind, give it to God and ask for his help. He will calm you and help you fight the worry.

God does this not because he has to but because he loves you.

67

Hope for When You're Tired

He gives strength to the weary
and increases the power of the weak.

ISAIAH 40:29

Sometimes you just get tired of fighting. It feels like life piles on one problem after another. It takes all your energy to get up in the morning and do what you have to do for the day. Maybe you work to put on a good front because of your Christianity. You don't want to let anyone know that you're struggling or hurting. After all, Christians aren't supposed to have problems, right? Wrong. Christians do have struggles, and it's not a negative testament to your faith when you do. On the contrary, struggles are inevitable, and they are an opportunity to reach out to God for help. They are a training ground to help your faith grow stronger.

When you ask God for help, he enhances your strength to keep on keeping on through whatever you're dealing with. God will give you strength to face each new day . . . one at a time. You probably won't experience a feeling of superhero strength, like you could fight off the world, but moment-by-moment and problem-by-problem, you'll have what you need. Trust God and thank him for his help.

68

Heartsongs of Music

I will sing to the LORD all my life;
I will sing praise to my God as long as I live.
May my meditation be pleasing to him,
as I rejoice in the LORD.

PSALM 104:33–34

Music can play an important role in your spiritual life. You might sing songs of joy when you're happy, silly songs when you feel goofy, and tender songs when you're sad. Music speaks to a place in the soul that plain words don't reach.

Sing out your praises to God! Sing loud and long, whether you can carry a tune or not. Sing thanks for his love for you, for his guidance, for his protection! Sing of his greatness and power! Sing your worship to him.

Sing your requests to God because you know he hears your musical prayers. Sing from the depths of pain in your heart. Sing your cries for rescue and your assurance of his hiding places. Sing because you know his Word to be true.

If there are no existing songs that say what you are feeling, make up your own. Just let your heart sing to him.

Sing to him all your life. Never let your songs of praise and love end. Know that he hears and he takes pleasure in your worship—in your joy and in your requests.

69

Hope for a Purposeful Life

Therefore, my dear friends, as you have always obeyed—not only in my presence, but now much more in my absence—continue to work out your salvation with fear and trembling, for it is God who works in you to will and to act in order to fulfill his good purpose.

PHILIPPIANS 2:12–13

Anything really worth having is worth working for. Think about when you start a diet, not just to lose weight but to be healthy too. When you first start, you're filled with enthusiasm and great intentions. But as time passes some of that enthusiasm fades, and it begins to feel like work to maintain a healthy diet. Still, in your heart you know that the goal of being healthy is a good one, and you should keep pushing through the discouragement and make it work.

What about learning to live for God in obedience and submission? When you first met Jesus, you probably enthusiastically embraced the new life he offered and vowed to learn and grow. But along the way you have encountered stumbling blocks and perhaps discouragement. The apostle Paul encourages you not to give up, because a life of obedience to God is worth having. That means it's worth diligently pursuing. God helps you to grow and learn because he has a purpose for your life, and through your obedience and growth, that purpose will become more obvious. A life of knowing and serving God creates a life of purpose and meaning.

70

Hope for Restoration

The God of all grace, who called you to his eternal glory in Christ, after you have suffered a little while, will himself restore you and make you strong, firm and steadfast.

1 PETER 5:10

Restored furniture is old furniture that has already lived a life but is given new life. It needs repair or a new coat of paint to make it usable and to give it a fresh look.

People need restoring sometimes too. The stresses of life can beat you down. Heavy problems bruise and wound you. You may come pretty close to being completely broken by what you deal with every day. The suffering may go on for a long time, and you may be tempted to lose hope of ever being out from under its crushing weight. But don't give up hope.

Why must you go through such pain? Only God knows. But you can know with certainty that you are never alone in your suffering. You belong to God, and he is paying attention to all that you're struggling with. Keep calling out to him and trusting him for help. Remember God's promise to rescue you and to restore you in strength and resilience so that you will have new life and usefulness to him.

71

Hope for Wisdom

The LORD gives wisdom;
from his mouth come knowledge and
understanding.

PROVERBS 2:6

How often have you mentally played back a conversation you've had and wondered whether you said the right thing . . . or realized that you didn't but wished you had known the right thing to say? If only you had wisdom to give great advice and always speak correctly to others. If only . . .

There's hope for you to gain wisdom. Your heavenly Father is wisdom itself. He created wisdom. His wisdom is available to you through studying his Word . . . ingesting it so that it becomes a part of your heart and thoughts. As you begin to live out his wisdom, it will become a part of your normal thoughts, and you can share it with others.

God's wisdom is different than the world's wisdom because of his ability to see the bigger picture of life and his focus on helping you learn to show his love to others. Ask him to give you his wisdom, and spend time in Scripture, letting his Word sink into your heart. That's how you have the hope of great wisdom to share with others, reflecting God's love to all.

72

Hope for Peace

Now may the Lord of peace himself give you peace at all times and in every way. The Lord be with all of you.

2 THESSALONIANS 3:16

Peace. Who doesn't want peace? But it's such a fleeting thing, so easily pushed away by anxious thoughts and conflicts. It seems that to be alive in these days is to be bombarded with less than peaceful situations and thoughts. The more people you care about, the more opportunities there are for peace to be distant as you see their struggles. The world is certainly not a peaceful place, and concern for its future can attack your personal peace too.

Is the reality of peace hopeless? No, it isn't, but it surely doesn't come without trusting God and asking him to help you see beyond your current crises. Echo the request in this verse for God to give you peace at all times and in every way. Be still and rest in him. Meditate on his Word. Give him your concerns, and every time you are tempted to grab them back so you can worry on them, give them to him again. He is always with you, loving you and caring for you. He himself is the essence of peace, and he will share that peace with you if you allow him to.

73

God's Best

To the faithful you show yourself faithful,
*   to the blameless you show yourself blameless,*
to the pure you show yourself pure,
*   but to the devious you show yourself shrewd.*
You save the humble
*   but bring low those whose eyes are haughty.*

PSALM 18:25–27

I t's a given fact that you do not deserve the grace of God or the gifts of his salvation and blessings. You are a sinner saved by grace, so your salvation and all the blessings he gives you are purely because of his grace and love.

His special blessings are given to those who accept Jesus as their Savior and who focus their energy on living for him and learning to know him in a deeper way. Those who are faithful to him see his faithfulness, those who obey him see his justice, and those who strive to be obedient see his grace.

But people who do not seek to obey or honor God will not, in the long run, see his kindness, only his judgment.

Do you hope to see more of God's goodness and blessing in your life? Then live humbly, giving him credit for all you are and all you have. Don't be filled with pride that pushes God aside and claims its own credit for all good things. If you hope to know God more deeply and enjoy his best, honor him and focus your life on knowing and obeying him.

74

Serving Jesus

Just as you received Christ Jesus as Lord, continue to live your lives in him, rooted and built up in him, strengthened in the faith as you were taught, and overflowing with thankfulness.

COLOSSIANS 2:6–7

When you are learning something new, such as how to drive a car, there's a learning curve until you've learned all you need to know to be ready to drive on your own. Even once you have your license, there are situations you must continue to learn how to maneuver through.

When you receive Jesus as your Savior, you hope for opportunities to serve him even though you don't yet know all you need to know about obeying God and serving him. The Christian life is a journey, so you keep learning and growing. But do you have to reach a certain point before you can feel that you are ready to serve him and actually call yourself a Christian? Of course not. From the moment you accept

Jesus, you are God's child and should begin serving him immediately.

It's true that life with Jesus is a journey and you will always be learning about him, but from the moment you accept him, you can begin telling others about his love. So don't put things on hold until you feel you've "arrived"; just get busy living for Jesus. As you serve him and grow more in love with him, your heart will overflow with thankfulness!

75

Hope for Defeating Fear

There is no fear in love. But perfect love drives out fear, because fear has to do with punishment. The one who fears is not made perfect in love.

1 JOHN 4:18

ear is crippling. It keeps you from taking risks, which keeps you from having new experiences. Fear can even keep you from doing the things you were once comfortable doing. Fear keeps you in a box where you think you're safe and protected, but it also prevents you from enjoying things you used to enjoy. Once fear has taken hold in your heart, it grows, making your fear spread to other areas.

How do you combat fear? Is there some way to push it away? This verse tells you that there is no fear in love. So your hope for getting rid of fear is to let God's love settle deep in your heart. Make his love your refuge so that any time fear begins to raise its ugly head, you can call on God to remind you of his powerful love. Fear and love cannot both reside in the same place. It's one or the other. If your heart is assured of God's love for you, then there is no room for fear. Your hope for overcoming fear is to realize God's love, accept it, believe it, and trust it.

76

Blessings of Obeying

*Blessed are those who keep his statutes
and seek him with all their heart.*

PSALM 119:2

The pathway to living for God is often called the straight and narrow. That sounds foreboding, like it's a way of living that's full of rules you have to keep, and that idea keeps some people from wanting to follow God. They think it sounds like their lives would be too limited and confined. That's a shame because living for God and walking the straight and narrow is not at all keeping a list of rules. God's way of living is life-giving because he asks you to live in a way that is good for your life and for the people around you. Living the way God directs makes your life more fulfilling and your relationships with others more pleasant. You learn to treat others with respect and kindness while still obeying and honoring God.

Keeping God's commandments and making the effort to know him in a deeper and more meaningful way lead to blessings from him. You'll experience the blessings of stronger faith, more confidence in your relationship with him, and a deeper understanding of his love for you and of his purpose for your life.

77

Hope for Sure Feet

The Sovereign LORD is my strength;
he makes my feet like the feet of a deer,
he enables me to tread on the heights.
HABAKKUK 3:19

$\mathcal{P}$icking your way through the struggles of life takes some skill. Sometimes you may feel like you're climbing a tall, rocky mountain, and every step you take puts you in danger of slipping from a ledge and plummeting down the mountainside.

However, when you call on the Lord to guide your steps, you have the hope of making it to the peak of the mountain, never once slipping. Your steps will be sure because God is directing you.

You know that God loves you and that his power and strength are greater than any situation you may encounter. He sees the entire picture of your life and knows what's ahead for you. He knows how this current struggle will end and what you can learn from it. Then why is it so difficult to trust him? Perhaps it's because it feels like you're stepping into the unknown. You can't see where you're going, and you're never sure that you're not going to slip. Your trust in God isn't strong enough. But each time you see his protection in your life, you will trust him a little more. His strength will make your steps sure. He won't let you fall.

78

Hope for Equipping

God is able to bless you abundantly, so that in all things at all times, having all that you need, you will abound in every good work.

2 CORINTHIANS 9:8

When God gives you a job to do, you may feel that you're not equipped. That you can't possibly do what he wants. There were a few people in the Bible who said "I can't" to God. They were wrong though, because when he asks you to do something, he gives you what you need to accomplish the task. He may not give all the skills at once but a step at a time, as you need them. All he wants you to do is accept the mission he gives you and trust him to bless you with what you need.

Do you desire to serve God? Do you hope to do amazing things for him? Then say yes to whatever he asks you to do, and trust him to supply whatever you need. Remember that he did that for Moses when he asked him to lead his people out of Egypt. He did that for Joshua when he asked him to capture Jericho. God's blessings are abundant, and he will give you all you need in order to do all he asks you to do. Don't be afraid. Don't be timid. Trust him.

79

Material Blessings?

Observe what the Lord your God requires: Walk in obedience to him, and keep his decrees and commands, his laws and regulations, as written in the Law of Moses. Do this so that you may prosper in all you do and wherever you go.

1 Kings 2:3

Of course you want to prosper in life. Who doesn't? There is the hope that as you mature, your life will get better, and you will have a higher income and a nicer home . . . a more comfortable life. But is that what this verse promises you? Is it saying that if you are obedient to God and follow his laws, he will give you more material things? No, it's not about material blessings at all.

Do you hope for God's best in your life? Then don't think about his best as financial blessings. God's best for you is better than money or nice homes or cars. It is for you to know him deeply and trust him more fully. Your relationship with him and your growth to become more like Christ are the most important things to him.

That's what this verse is saying—obey God. Keep his commands and laws. Then you are honoring and obeying him and learning to be more like Christ—obedient to God, a humble servant, loving others more than yourself. If you live that way, you will indeed prosper in God's sight and receive his blessing of more opportunities to serve him.

80

Hope in Nourishment

Blessed is the one who trusts in the LORD,
whose confidence is in him.
They will be like a tree planted by the water
that sends out its roots by the stream.
It does not fear when heat comes;
its leaves are always green.
It has no worries in a year of drought
and never fails to bear fruit.

JEREMIAH 17:7–8

In a time of drought, plants and trees starve. As the drought persists, water dries up, and even trees with deep roots begin to struggle to get enough nourishment. But a tree that's even somewhat near a river will send its roots out toward the stream until it can locate water so the entire tree can get what it needs to survive. The whole tree—trunk, branches, and leaves—depends on the work of the roots to survive.

Your trust in God is your only hope of survival in a world that continuously tries to pull you away from him. Putting your trust in him over anything else is like a tree root seeking water from a stream and supplying all the needs of the entire plant. Your trust in God gives you everything you need to resist the temptations of Satan. It gives you the nourishment to grow in your faith, and it feeds your strength to love others and to live humbly before God. You just can't do all of this in your own strength. Your energy will dry up, and you will die. Only with the nourishment of trusting God can you survive.

81

Hope from Discipline

Blessed is the one whom God corrects.
JOB 5:17

Being corrected is no fun. Correction is discipline, and you're only disciplined when you've done something wrong. When you disobey a rule that your parents gave you or the rules of the road when you're driving, you are subject to discipline. It's not a bad thing to be disciplined; it helps you remember to obey the rules, and that makes life in the family more pleasant and the roads and highways safer.

In your hope to grow more like Christ there will be times when God disciplines you. His discipline takes various forms. Sometimes it comes through another Christian challenging you about choices you're making. Sometimes it comes through lost opportunities. Sometimes it comes through a feeling deep in your heart.

It's important to remember that God only disciplines you because he loves you. He wants very good things for you, and he knows that it's necessary for you to obey him and follow his Word in order to have the best life possible.

So if you hope for the best life with God, accept his discipline, learn what you must from it, move forward with the new lesson learned, and thank him for his love that cares enough to discipline.

82

Hope for the Faithful

These were all commended for their faith, yet none of them received what had been promised, since God had planned something better for us so that only together with us would they be made perfect.

Hebrews 11 lists great heroes of the faith and records the amazing ways they honored God by their faith in him. Their inspirational stories provide wonderful examples of trusting God and living for him. God was pleased with them, and he made sure they were included in this Hall of Faith chapter.

Interestingly, none of them were immediately rewarded for their lives of faith. They lived obedient lives and served God, yet they didn't get the reward God promised. Why not? Because their stories wouldn't be complete without yours. Their faith and your faith come together for a beautiful reward in heaven. You learn from the way they served God, and they are witnesses to how you serve him. They are the crowd of witnesses in heaven watching your faith and trust in God grow stronger and stronger! Your life of faith makes theirs more complete, and theirs make yours complete. So you will share in the grand reward of heaven together with them. How wonderful to be part of the entire family of God.

83

Hope in God Showing Up

The sun stopped in the middle of the sky and delayed going down about a full day. There has never been a day like it before or since, a day when the LORD listened to a human being. Surely the LORD was fighting for Israel!

JOSHUA 10:13–14

Joshua's army was fighting a battle that he really wanted to win, so he asked God to make the sun stand still—to prolong the daylight hours so his army could defeat God's enemies. What an amazing request. What's even more amazing is that God did it! He made the sun stand still in the sky so Joshua's army could defeat their enemies. As these verses say, that had never happened before and has never happened since.

Do you need God's help with something so big you know there is no other hope for a way to handle it, no logical way for the problem to be solved? It's going to take God's miraculous strength to deal with it. Do you dare ask him for a miracle? Will he hear your request?

You have the certain hope of God hearing what you ask. How he chooses to handle your crisis is, of course, up to him, but you can be assured he will hear and he will help. You never know how God will show up for you, but you can always be certain that he will show up in some way, and it will be exciting!

84

Hope in Your Importance to God

The very hairs of your head are all numbered. Don't be afraid; you are worth more than many sparrows.

LUKE 12:7

Do you feel that perhaps your requests are too small and unimportant compared to what others deal with? God has so much to take care of. Really—there are wars around the world, people dying from thirst or starvation, children suffering. Homeless people and sick veterans must take up a lot of God's time. There are massive storms and earthquakes and then the everyday occurrences of illness, death, or broken relationships. He is constantly bombarded with cries for help.

Maybe God doesn't need to be bothered with your problems. Of course you know he loves you, but maybe you feel you shouldn't ask him to handle your mundane requests.

It may be tempting to feel that way, but it isn't true. God is big enough to handle all the problems of the world and to hear every prayer as it is being uttered. He cares about you. He cares so much that he has counted the very hairs on your head! You're worth that much to him! So ask him what you need to ask him. Tell him what you want to tell him. Bask in his love and care for you.

85

Where Is Your Treasure?

Do not store up for yourselves treasures on earth, where moths and vermin destroy, and where thieves break in and steal. But store up for yourselves treasures in heaven, where moths and vermin do not destroy, and where thieves do not break in and steal. For where your treasure is, there your heart will be also.

MATTHEW 6:19–21

You may say all the right words about loving and honoring God, and that is good. But words without action behind them are just that—words. You need more than words to show where your heart is truly focused. Where do you put your time? Where do you invest your finances? What takes up most of your thoughts and conversations? Those things indicate where your treasure is. They are the proof of what's truly important to you.

Your hope is the certainty of heaven where you will spend eternity. What you invest in that future will be your reward. Do you need to take a step back and evaluate where your treasure really is? Be careful about what's important to you here on earth. You won't get a chance to redo those time and energy investments once you leave this earth. Show God that he is truly your priority. Invest your energy, time, finances, thoughts—everything—in his work on earth. Your heart will then be focused on serving and honoring him, and your treasure will be in heaven.

86

Praise to Almighty God!

To him who is able to keep you from stumbling and to present you before his glorious presence without fault and with great joy—to the only God our Savior be glory, majesty, power and authority, through Jesus Christ our Lord, before all ages, now and forevermore! Amen.

JUDE 24–25

The only hope you have to make it through the struggles of this life and stay true to God is to call on him for help. He can keep you from giving in to temptation that would pull you away from living for him. His strength in you can keep you true to obeying him. His power and authority will defeat any other power or person on earth. He is God Almighty, and because you are his child, that power is available to you for the asking. You need only to be submissive to his guidance and to his plan for your life.

The blessing of that hope is that you will one day stand before him fault-free, your sin cleaned up by the blood of

Jesus, and God himself will celebrate with joy because you are there with him.

So praise him now! Praise God for his glory, majesty, power, and authority over everything! Praise him for his unending, unconditional, sacrificial love for you! His love is the reason you can have any hope at all. It gives you hope for all eternity.

87

Hope in Keeping On

I want to know Christ—yes, to know the power of his resurrection and participation in his sufferings, becoming like him in his death, and so, somehow, attaining to the resurrection from the dead. Not that I have already obtained all this, or have already arrived at my goal, but I press on to take hold of that for which Christ Jesus took hold of me.

PHILIPPIANS 3:10–12

Keep on keeping on. That's the message Paul shares. Keep on keeping on toward the goal you hope for. What's important to you? What are you willing to sacrifice, to leave behind, to suffer for? You won't keep pressing toward a goal if it's not the most important thing to you.

Hopefully you, like Paul, are pressing toward achieving the goal Christ has set for you. He wants your full submission—a heart and mind that are totally dedicated to him and willing to obey, regardless of how difficult it sometimes is. He wants your attitude of service to be "I'll go where you want me to go, and I'll do what you want me to do." Is that your attitude even when you don't understand why he is asking you to do something or to go somewhere? Do you trust him enough to step out in darkness, knowing he will set your feet on solid ground?

Faith is a day-by-day journey. It's a learning process and not one that comes quickly or easily. You must commit to it every day—sometimes multiple times a day—in order to keep your eyes on the goal of knowing and serving God.

88

Hope in His Protection

You are my refuge and my shield;
I have put my hope in your word.
PSALM 119:114

God is your refuge—your place of protection from danger and wickedness. He goes before you, he comes behind you, he hems you in on all sides. He is your shield against all attacks. Satan tries everything he can think of to discourage your connection to God and to convince you that God doesn't care about you, that he doesn't matter, or even that he isn't real. Your mind knows it's not true, but sometimes your heart needs a respite from the doubts. Let God shield you while the bruises on your heart heal and your strength to stand for him returns.

Think about a shield as a deflector. When someone shoots unkind, critical words at you that make you doubt your worth, the shield of the truth of God's Word deflects them away from your heart. The truth of who he says you are to him is protected. God's Word is truth, and what you learn from it will help you to know God better and to guide you in living for him.

Your hope for safety and protection is in God and his Word. Keep them at the forefront of your thoughts at all times.

89

Hope in Community

*Though one may be overpowered,
two can defend themselves.
A cord of three strands is not quickly broken.*

ECCLESIASTES 4:12

It's a good thing to have friends, and it's a blessing to have the right friends. The right friends are those who share your faith in Jesus and who will hold you accountable to living for him. They aren't afraid to challenge you about choices you make or whether you're living your life in obedience to God's Word. This kind of friend will stand with you against attacks from others or from Satan himself. Holding each other up in prayer and with words of encouragement gives you the power and strength to stand against all kinds of attacks. Together you are twice as strong. Your bond of friendship and faith is unbreakable.

Three cords are referred to in this verse. You and your friend are two of the cords. What's the third cord? Christ himself! He is always standing with you against attacks and in the battles of life. God in his wisdom knows that while Christ is enough, sometimes you need someone with skin on to stand next to you and hold you up with words of encouragement and pats on the back. In this way, you and your friend are braided together with Christ. That is a cord that nothing and no one can break!

90

Hope for a Rich Life

The love of money is a root of all kinds of evil. Some people, eager for money, have wandered from the faith and pierced themselves with many griefs.

1 TIMOTHY 6:10

Money isn't evil. If God has blessed you with a goodly amount of it, then praise him! Use it to do good things for his kingdom and his people. But . . . don't *love* money. When you love money more than you love God, working to get more money becomes most important. You may even be tempted to cheat or steal to get more money. That's where wandering from the faith comes in. Those who put their focus on money push aside living for God and obeying him. They forget about helping those who don't have enough to live on and about God's work around the world that needs financial support. They focus their generosity where a tax write-off is involved so their "generosity" benefits them.

If you are money focused, you're hurting yourself. You will, in the long run, cause yourself grief by your disobedience to God. You will answer to him for it.

Make knowing and serving God the most important thing in your life. Live generously with all he gives you. You will have the hope of the reward you gain. To hear "Well done, my good and faithful servant" is worth more than money in the bank!

Carolyn Larsen is the bestselling author of more than fifty books for children and adults. She has been a speaker for women's events and classes around the world, bringing scriptural messages filled with humor and tenderness. For more information, visit carolynlarsen.com and follow her on Facebook.